"Maeley Tom's contributions far transcend the Asian American and Pacific Islander community and permeate the diversity of our nation."

— SENATOR ART TORRES (RET.), Former chair of the California Democratic Party, 1996-2009

"Maeley is an amazing story teller—taking the reader on a behind the scenes lifetime journey that transforms California and national politics and empowers the entire Asian American community. It's about how one person who could have been a victim overcomes every hurdle thrown at her to be the heroine of her own life, and becomes a beloved and trusted mentor to generations of name recognizable leaders. You won't be able to stop reading this incredible saga; you can't help but become a better person after you've finished."

— GINGER LEW, Former White House advisor to President Obama

"...a compelling story of a smart, strong Asian American woman who overcame a parentless childhood and a major political scandal to forge a stellar place in American public life."

— WILLIAM GEE WONG, Author, *Yellow Journalist: Dispatches from Asian America*

"Maeley is a true warrior with significant battle scars who never loses sight of community and purpose. I couldn't stop reading."

— ASSEMBLYMAN EVAN LOW, Campbell, California

D1707352

"…a clear-eyed but touching memoir, a guide book on how the inner workings of government in the country's most progressive state grind along…An awesome, very human achievement."

— ED GOLDMAN, syndicated columnist and author of *Don't Cry for Me, Ardent Reader*

"Maeley has been a trailblazer in breaking the Asian American glass ceiling in public service, and an inspiring mentor and counselor…"

— BUCK GEE, Former senior executive with Cisco Systems, and author of: Asian Americans are the least likely group in the U.S. to be promoted. *Harvard Business Review*

"… a unique insider perspective from a pioneering Asian American woman in the rough and tumble world of California and national politics. Her grit, perseverance, and dedication are an inspiration to us all."

— TIMOTHY P. FONG, PH.D., Professor, Department of Ethnic Studies, California State University, Sacramento

"…required reading for every Asian Pacific Islander school kid, showing the heroic efforts of one woman who successfully lifted Asian Pacific Islanders into California's political mainstream… an inspiration to all of us who value the diversity of our great American experience."

— DAVID TOWNSEND, California political consultant

I'M NOT WHO YOU THINK I AM

An Asian American
Woman's Political Journey

MAELEY TOM

For more information, address: rtom902677@aol.com

ISBN: 9798649915885

Editing by Bob Magnuson and Laurie Hensley
Cover and interior design by Vanessa Perez

DEDICATION

*To my husband Ron for teaching me the
meaning of love*

*To my daughter Stephanie for being the
woman and mother I wish I could have been*

*To my grandson Maxwell for bringing so
much joy into my life*

IN MEMORY OF

Marianne "Mama" Itcague

TABLE OF CONTENTS

ACKNOWLEDGEMENTS

To Georgette Imura, whose friendship changed my life, I thank you for always being the "wind beneath my wings."

I also thank and acknowledge every individual who contributed and participated in putting together the two historic Asian Pacific Islander Americans (APIA) Democratic leadership conferences at the state and national level as noted in the appendix of this book. During this era, each individual represented grass root groups fighting to ensure that the presence of Asian Pacific Islander American groups was recognized in this diverse country.

A special thank you to the Honorable Norman Mineta and former California APIA Legislative Caucus Chair Mike Honda for devoting their lives to enhancing the political roles of APIA in state legislatures and in Congress.

I had amazing role models after whom I tried to pattern my life, such as Ginger Lew, Dale Minami, Ron Wakabayashi, Henry Der, former Ambassador Linda Tsao Yang, and the late Alice Bulos, the matriarch of Filipino Democratic politics. They were all fearless trailblazers who gained recognition and respect as they broke barriers and challenged injustice and discrimination. And to the late famous Sacramento restaurateur Frank Fat and wife Mary, thank you for including me in your family as your goddaughter.

As the beneficiary of many mentors, I especially thank the late Assembly Rules Chairman Lou Papan and the late Senator John Vasconcellos who deeply influenced my life as well as my career. And to David Townsend and former State Senator Art Torres, I am so blessed that our political relationships turned into four decades of friendship and love. And to Congresswoman Maxine Waters, thank you for always being there when I needed you.

In the book, I have acknowledged and still see many friends who were my surrogate family from childhood through high school and college and throughout my professional career. And yet so much of my adult personal life has been enriched by a sisterhood of women who have played significant roles in my personal journey for decades such as Dorinda Lee Ng, my longest living friend from my days with "Mama;" Faye Kishimori, my soul sister in Hawaii; and my Sacramento sisters who embraced me when I returned to Sacramento to marry Ron, Nanci Jan and the late Lina Fat.

This book would not have been possible without the encouragement of authors Helen Zia, William Gee Wong, and Ed Goldman and the coaching of communication gurus Bobbie Metzger, Barbara O'Connor, and Lynn Choy Uyeda. Buck Gee, thank you for the suggested title.

I am not sure I could have completed this book if it were not for Bob Magnuson, my editor. He deserves a medal for his patience in coping with my computer challenged skills. His compassion and insight into how I could accurately portray the experiences in this book were invaluable. I also thank my guiding angels Laurie Hensley and Vanessa Perez for their guidance in getting this book published.

As we go to print, the COVID 19 pandemic has exposed how vulnerable our community is to being a scapegoat, merely based on hateful anti-China rhetoric perpetuated by the current administration of this country. The resulting surge of hate crimes and assaults against Asian Americans are proof.

However, there is some solace in that Asian Americans are fighting back through their organizational institutions, their use of social media, their formation of alliances with other groups, such as the NAACP and the Anti Defamation League, and proudly through the voices of Asian American elected officials who now serve in numbers large enough to make a difference. Congresswoman Grace Meng (D-New York) just introduced a resolution in Congress to denounce anti-Asian sentiment caused by corona virus, and it has attracted 124 cosponsors to date.

Although we now have a voice, the battle continues for us to be fully recognized as Americans, not foreigners.

BOOK ONE

I begin…

"In life you have two names: the name with which you are born, and the one that you make for yourself."
—Anonymous

PROLOGUE

It is 1997. I am one of the targets involved in the Clinton Asian fundraising scandal. It has rocked the nation. Headlines allege illegal foreign donors from Asia had been trying to influence U.S. policy as agents from China.

My personal ordeal overwhelms me emotionally—but even more distressing is the daily bashing by the media and Congress, bashing that reinforces the image of all Asians being "foreigners" and not to be trusted. It's as though we're back in the United States of World War II, when the image of an Asian face—whether Japanese, Chinese, or Vietnamese—in a film or photograph, a face that had once suggested exotica, now suggested evil. My people had once again become a stereotype, fifty-two years after the war had ended.

At the time, my attorney, Nancy Luque, tells me I should consider writing a book about this national scandal that is victimizing an entire ethnic community—when, in fact, there are many other cases of more egregious illegal contributions from other foreign countries, cases that are barely noticed in Congress or mentioned by the press.

Her suggestion gives me the strength to get through this scandal by making me promise myself that someday I will indeed write about this episode. I want what I write to memorialize another case of prejudice and discriminatory treatment of the Asian American community in this country. It also will allow me to absolve some of the individuals who have been tainted by this scandal.

As I began to write this book, I realize my life as a non-elected Asian American woman working behind the scenes in politics has provided me with many unique opportunities and unforgettable experiences, incidents that have included many high-profile political figures, including presidential candidates, at a time when Asian Americans were just awakening politically. I decided to also share those stories.

...

My professional and political careers in California and Asian American politics have been well recognized among my community and the Democratic establishment through the years. However, I have not been as open about my personal and family background—which in many ways played a role in how I navigated my professional journey.

Very few people in my life were aware of my unusual upbringing as a child born to parents who were Cantonese Opera performers—definitely not your typical Asian immigrant parents who strive to help their children succeed as Asian Americans.

In my case, my parents were a part of a world of self-indulgence and fame and lived a lifestyle that left no time for raising a family. These circumstances provided me with an unusual childhood that I have kept more or less hidden for all these years.

Now that I have become more accepting of myself, surviving years of doubt and need for self validation through perseverance and determination, I've decided to share this part of my life in this book. My hope is that my story will inspire those who have faced similar barriers to never allow "being different" to deter them from achieving their dreams.

A note of clarity: as you read this book, you will see that I have used different designations for various ethnic groups, depending on the context. I refer to myself, as well as many colleagues, as Asian American, as it describes personal background. In other contexts, I use Asian Pacific Islander Americans (APIA) for the sake of full inclusion of all sub-ethnic groups. In some chapters I just used the word Asian Americans, because neither Filipino Americans nor Pacific Islander Americans were part of those particular events. I have also used the word Asian immigrants to identify these individuals as separate from Asian American citizens.

This book opens my past as well as the experiences I faced trying to overcome the cultural stereotype of an Asian American woman in the male-dominated political world.

In short, it reveals that "I am not the person you think I am." And I hope it helps you discover, or rediscover, the person you are.

WHO AM I?

I was not born into a traditional family. Certainly not by American standards. Not even by Chinese American norms.

My parents immigrated to this country in the late 1930s from Guangzhou, China, under a special visa for members of a Cantonese Opera troupe. The opera sprang up in San Francisco during the 1850s when Chinese immigrants primarily from the southern part of China left their homes to join the gold rush in California known as Gum San, or mountain of gold.

As these immigrants arrived seeking the American dream, they instead experienced hatred and racial violence, causing them to seek refuge in their own neighborhood—especially in San Francisco, known today to be the home of the first Chinatown in the country.

The most popular form of entertainment in San Francisco's Chinatown at that time was the Cantonese Opera, where these new immigrants could find an escape from the harsh living conditions of their new world and maintain an emotional connection to their homeland.

My father, Luk Wun Fay, was a popular comedian with the opera troupe. My mother, Lee Chor Fun, was an opera singer. My parents' families were descendants of generations of performers of Cantonese Opera. The only education or training my parents received as children was to master the art of the Cantonese Opera as a singer or stage performer.

In San Francisco they lived the fast, hard lives of entertainers in a world Anglos rarely saw.

My mother sang nightly in the gambling dens; my father performed on stage every evening until midnight. After the show, the partying began and went on into the wee hours. Gambling, eating, drinking, and socializing with their clique of opera performers consumed their off-stage hours. Then, they slept until mid-afternoon, rising in time to memorize their lines for that night's show.

Housing and meals were subsidized by the theater owner, who also secured the performers' visas and paid for travel from China to the United States. My father's troupe lived in a tenement in the alley adjacent to the San Francisco Chinese Hospital on Jackson Street.

Each performer had a 500 sq. ft. apartment with a bedroom and living room. The performers shared one bathroom on each floor. Everyone cooked and ate together in a communal kitchen and dining room before heading out to the Dai Mo Toy theatre on Grant Avenue. Before the curtain rose at 8 p.m., there were hours spent on ritual Kabuki-style makeup and hair styles and planning the costumes each performer was to wear.

After the four-hour performance came the ritual midnight meal—suey yeah—at any number of Chinatown establishments. Then came the gambling dens to finish off the night.

This was the life of the Cantonese Opera performer, seven days a week with only the rare day off. It was a tight-knit group, an intimate circle of artists, a self-sustaining social system requiring little outside interaction. There was no need to learn English. These people were Chinatown celebrities with plenty of local Chinese American-born groupies hanging around backstage to drive them, speak for them, and cater to their needs if actors wanted to venture out of their comfort zone and into white society. They were the "beautiful people" of San Francisco's Chinatown.

This became my world.

I recall my mother telling me that in 1940, the year before I was born, there was an actor called Lee Hoi Cherng who lived with his wife directly above my parents' apartment. On his way to the theatre one night, Lee asked my mother, who had a day off, to please look after his very pregnant wife. Later, my mother heard a loud thumping noise from above and ran upstairs to help her friend, heavy in labor, walk to the Chinese Hospital around the corner. That night, the woman gave birth to a son she named Lee Jun Fan, which means "to return again." Lee Jun Fan's name was changed to Lee Suey Loong, which means "Little Dragon," when he entered the theatre arts in Hong Kong. But we all came to know him as Bruce Lee, one of the greatest martial artists of his generation. He died much too soon and our lives never crossed paths.

...

My entrance into the world was perhaps less auspicious. But dark.

My parents had one daughter in China who was being raised by my mother's sister. My sister died of yellow fever at age 12. My parents were not prepared to have another child while in the U.S. However, after three abortions, my mother acquiesced to my father's pleas to go through with the pregnancy. He wanted another child, hopefully a son, to carry on his family name. Unfortunately, my mother went into labor during a citywide blackout in San Francisco imposed three days after the attack on Pearl Harbor. A very superstitious gambler, my mother quickly deemed my birth a sign of bad luck. The lights went out just as I arrived.

My father rushed to the hospital immediately after his performance, accompanied by his only English-speaking friend,

Henry Chang. Chang, a merchant marine, became the unofficial translator for the opera troupe after he befriended the performers on the ship that brought them to San Francisco.

When the English-speaking nurse asked who the father was, my dad pointed to Henry to answer the question; Henry pointed to my dad to identify him as the father. The nurse understandably was befuddled. "You better decide between the two of you who the father is so I can complete the birth certificate," she demanded. (Henry Chang subsequently became my godfather and related this story to me.)

As for a name, once again the language barrier played a starring role. My father liked Mary, but with his Chinese accent it came out Maly. The frustrated nurse spelled it the way she heard it: Maeley. My father never learned English and therefore never knew the difference; as far as he was concerned, I was Mary.

Two weeks later, my parents followed the example of most of their fellow opera performers who either sent their children to be raised in China or sent them to a local foster care home. Realizing their lifestyle was not conducive to raising an infant who required regular feedings, diaper changes, and constant attention, my parents sent me to live in the Richmond District with a French Basque woman in her 50s whom I fondly called "Mama," Marieanne "Mama" Itcague.

· · ·

From the age of two weeks old I was raised by this lovely "Mama" and her husband, "Papa," first-generation immigrants. Papa was a gardener by occupation, and they had an adult daughter, Justine, who helped Mama with her child-care business.

Mama was well known among San Francisco Chinese families for her rare ability to care for young children suffering from severe skin rashes such as eczema, which were common among Chinese infants and toddlers. San Francisco's famous Chinese American pediatrician, Dr. Stanley Louie, referred many of his patients to her. A fellow actor in the troupe, Wong Chew Mo, and his wife boarded their young son Mason with Mama and referred my parents to her.

At first, when I tell people my first eight years were spent in foster care, I get a sad, sympathetic glance. But in reality, these years were among my happiest. I did not miss my own parents; Mama's home became the only home I knew. Oddly perhaps, I flourished in a European-dominated Richmond neighborhood with cultural attitudes that encouraged self-expression, the open display of affection, and strong self-esteem among the children.

Mama loved to brag to her European neighbors about her smart Chinese kids.

She would tell them how I started walking at nine months, talked at a very early age, and mimicked songs on the radio by age two. While I was growing up, Mama reinforced in me that I was unusually smart. During my grammar school years at George Peabody School, I skipped two full grades.

When I was three-and-a-half years old, Mama sent me to the Anderson Sisters Dancing School two blocks away at 7th Avenue and Clement. I was the youngest regular performer at the annual shows for the U.S. Armed Forces at the San Francisco Civic Auditorium during World War II. Even at that early age, I recall loving the attention and applause I received for singing "Gimme a Little Kiss" before an audience of over 1,000 soldiers. No, I was not shy.

Most of the young children under Mama's care only stayed with her during the work week. This was true for my lifelong friend, Dorinda Lee Ng. Her parents worked full-time jobs and picked up Dorinda and her sister, Rosalind, every weekend. Dorinda's father, Lim P. Lee, led an extremely active life at work and in politics. Later, he became the first Asian American U.S. Postmaster and the San Francisco Chinatown post office is named after him.

Regular parental weekend visits were not a priority for our celebrity parents. More often than not, Mason and I would remain with Mama while the other children went home with their parents on weekends. Mama always made sure she planned something special for Mason and me so we would have something to look forward to on weekends and not feel left behind. We were also the only kids who spent holidays with Mama's family because our parents were usually performing. Once in a while, our moms or dads would surprise us with a trip to Chinatown for the weekend. But both Mason's and my parents separated from each other soon after and neither of us has memories of his parents and mine together with us.

Sometime during my infancy, my mother left my father to sing in the gambling dens of Seattle. Mason and I stayed with Mama even after most of the other children left the house to return home to attend grammar school. Still, we did not feel neglected or deprived; as far as we were concerned, Mama's house was our home and her special love and generosity more than compensated for our lack of parental attention.

At six years of age, I was devastated when Mason, who was two years older, went to live with his mother in New York. He teased me as he left, joking that I was the last one left at Mama's house while he was happily reuniting with mother. Sadly, though, I came to find out that his mother had no intention of caring for Mason on a permanent basis; not long after, she sent him to stay at the Chung Mei home for boys.

Mason and I saw one another from time to time but were not in close touch until he moved to San Francisco, married Maggie, and had two sons, Matthew and Marcus. Now we consider each other family because of what we went through together in those very early years. The experiences we shared at Mama's house forever sealed the bond between us as brother and sister.

. . .

I stayed with Mama for two more years.

My mother assumed financial custody of my care when my father left for China. Upon my mother's return to San Francisco, she decided I should live in Chinatown and learn to speak Chinese. At the age of eight I was suddenly torn away from the only family and security I had known. I was frightened and did not want to leave.

Looking back, the eight years I spent at Mama's house were an extraordinary gift. During the most formative years of my life, I was in the care of a loving, warm, supportive caretaker. And growing up in a non-Asian environment freed me from the traditional cultural barriers that often work against Asians struggling to get by in Western society. I learned invaluable social skills early on, which enabled me later to thrive and advance in professional situations that demanded social skills and personality traits that conformed to Western cultural mores and perceptions of success and achievement.

The strength and character Mama instilled helped steel me for the turmoil that lay ahead as I faced the world on my own. To this day, I feel the life-affirming influence of the French Basque culture every time I greet friends with a big hug and warm embrace.

. . .

Mother and father, wedding picture; Father and me at Mama's house; Me, 3 1/2 years old at dancing school; Mama and baby David Wong, me, and Mason; Mason Wong and me at Mama's house

CHINATOWN NIGHTMARE/ OAKLAND REFUGE

"Turn your wounds into wisdom." —Oprah Winfrey

When I was preparing to leave Mama's house after eight years, I found some fleeting comfort in thinking I was going to finally live a normal life with my real mother.

I was wrong.

My mother had no intention of living together for the simple reason—cruel in my eyes—that it wasn't conducive to the glamourous, seemingly carefree lifestyle she'd created for herself. Instead, she sent me to live with a family directly across the street from the one-bedroom apartment she shared with her latest boyfriend, on Powell and Broadway across from Jean Parker Elementary school.

Harvey Lum was a widower who employed a fulltime caretaker, Pearl Chew, for his young adult daughter, Eunice, and teenage son, Eugene. Uncle Harvey was the general manager of the Club Shanghai nightclub. I moved in with this family and Auntie Pearl became my new caretaker.

The only silver lining to this arrangement was that on weekends my mother would take me to the Chinese Opera where I would hang out backstage with my "theatre family." I loved being at the theatre because I was with all my dad's friends, which brought back happy memories.

The transition from Mama's house in the Richmond district to Chinatown with a strange family was unbearable at first; I cried every night for over a month. However, as I adjusted to my new surroundings, I came to appreciate being close to the theatre, absorbing the Chinese culture, eating Chinese food, and being surrounded by so many people who looked like me. I enjoyed learning how to read, write, and speak the Cantonese language at St. Mary's Chinese School and hearing Cantonese as the spoken language around Chinatown.

I remember Auntie Pearl enjoyed taking care of me and liked dressing me up in the best school clothes and curling my hair every morning. However, for some reason, Eugene hated me from the day I moved in. He would call me "Fatso," and used every opportunity to make my life miserable when there was no one to come to my aid. Fortunately, attending regular school during the day and Chinese school afterward limited my being alone with Eugene.

Though Auntie Pearl would try, she couldn't protect me from Eugene's bullying. He got away with it because his father refused to discipline him. Eugene had been spoiled ever since his mother had died at a very young age.

I was terrified of Eugene—but a far more serious danger was Auntie Pearl's nephew, David, an unemployed ex-sailor in his early 20s who volunteered to babysit me whenever Auntie Pearl had an evening Mahjong game. Little did Auntie Pearl know that David would wake me up in the middle of the night to show me pictures of Chinese men and women having sex. He never forced himself on me, but he would try to fondle me and make me touch his exposed penis. At the age of eight, I didn't know anything about sex, but my instincts told me what he was doing was wrong. When

I resisted and cried, he told me not to tell anyone or they would label me a "bad girl."

After several terrifying incidents I finally told Auntie Pearl I did not want David to be my babysitter. I didn't tell her why. Finally, during one of my visits with my mother, I broke down and told her about David, looking for protection and hoping she would take me to live with her. Instead, my mother lost her highly volatile temper. She accused me of lying and making up excuses so I could return to Mama's house.

I felt betrayed and could barely speak. What made matters worse, my mother told Auntie Pearl. After that, I was treated like a pariah by everyone in the Harvey Lum household.

This meant Eugene had license to hit me openly any time he wanted. All I could do was to try to hide or stay out of his way. But I took solace in the fact that David was never allowed to baby sit me again, suggesting that someone must have believed me after all.

Thankfully, my time in Chinatown was short-lived. The only semblance of normalcy during those two years were my school friends at Jean Parker Elementary, who never had an inkling of what my life was like at home because I was never allowed to bring friends to the house. Nor could I visit them. And I never discussed any of it; I just wanted to be "normal" like the other kids*.

Reflecting back, this was a life-changing transition from a loving, stable home with Mama to a life of abuse by a family of strangers. These often-terrifying experiences helped crystalize my growing awareness that the only person I could depend on was myself. I was completely alone. This realization forced me to survive by becoming self-reliant. The only positive result of this experience was that I enjoyed my new identity and the culture of being a Chinese American.

By chance, at a wedding 60 years later, I was reunited with Cara Jang, one of my dearest friends at Jean Parker Elementary. We tearfully embraced as she told me she never knew what happened to me, because after a summer break I never returned to school, and she had no way to get in touch. My mother's abrupt plans to move to Oakland with her new boyfriend, Uncle Ed, during summer vacation did not give me a chance to say goodbye to my school friends at Jean Parker. Cara said she later followed my career through my *Asian Week* articles. She and my other friends at Jean Parker never knew how much I cherished their friendship at the time. It was my only positive memory of those dark years.

...

At age 10, I finally got the chance to live with my mother—this time in Oakland with her new boyfriend, Uncle Ed Ong.

Our home was in a predominantly Chinese neighborhood, walking distance from the Oakland Chinatown and Lincoln School.

Uncle Ed was a private, quiet, kind, and gentle man. He was influential around Chinatown where he managed the underground gambling dens.

Uncle Ed was already married with a family in China and my mother was his second "wife." He decided to move his legal wife and their two adult sons from China to live in Oakland with my mom and me under one roof. At the time it was not unusual for wealthy Chinese immigrant men to have more than one wife and family, but it was highly unusual for multiple families to live together under one roof.

Upon arrival, my two adult stepbrothers, Calvin and Raymond, entered college and then the Armed Services. Eventually, both married Chinese wives and started their own families. As for my mother and me, we rarely saw one another even though we were in the same house. She slept during the days and awoke with just enough time to cook dinner for everyone before she left for her nightly Mahjong games. The only time we spent together was when she would take me to her weekend games. She was cold and our interactions impersonal, with her reminding me of my missed household chores. We rarely talked like mother and daughter.

She never asked me about school or grades or my neighborhood friends. But she seemed to implicitly trust me and was quite liberal about the amount of time I spent with my friends away from home.

After years of hostile tension between my mother and Uncle Ed's legal wife, he and my mother moved back to San Francisco. I was 14 when my mother gave me the choice of going with her or staying in Oakland to finish high school.

By this time, I had finally found friends I could bond with, a neighborhood peer group that spanned my days at Lincoln School, Westlake Jr. High and then Oakland Technical High: Jeri Yip Oh, Lainey Lee Wong, Elaine Hom Wong, Lucy Ng Ozawa, Lonnie Moy Walker, and the late Sarah Fong Torres Watkins. My friends meant more to me than living with my own mother, so I chose to stay in Oakland even if it meant living alone with Uncle Ed's first wife, who really wanted nothing to do with me.

This left me pretty much on my own from that day forward.

Uncle Ed's wife mostly stayed in her room, coming out only to eat by herself or visit with her two sons. I felt sorry for her because she was isolated and alone, with limited language skills and no friends, and my mother was living across the bay with her husband. Raymond and Calvin were always very cordial when they visited; they seemed to understand that this awkward living arrangement was not my fault.

Uncle Ed visited once a week and gave me a generous monthly allowance. Between studies and attending school, I used my allowance to take care of my daily needs, school expenses, clothes and meals which were usually Swanson TV dinners and *lop cheung* (Chinese sausage) over rice. I had plenty of money left over to spend on activities with friends during the weekends.

On weekends, I hung out with my neighborhood friends without any adult supervision. When it came to dating, I forced myself to follow the same rules parents of my peer group imposed because I wanted my behavior and conduct to meet their standards.

I never had time to feel sorry for myself. My neighborhood friends treated me simply as "one of the group" despite my unconventional living situation, and this gave me a sense of belonging and normalcy that made it easier to be on my own.

The times I missed family were during traditional holidays.

My mother and Uncle Ed did not celebrate birthdays, Easter, Thanksgiving or Christmas. The Tong family downstairs from the flat where I lived were good friends of Uncle Ed and they had a daughter, Frances, and two sons, Johnny and Willie, whom I played with when I first moved to Oakland. They were always so kind and generous to invite me to join their family on such occasions.

But there were times when I just preferred to be on my own. I did not want to intrude. I had my pride.

Oakland Tech High School became the center of my life. I was very active in student activities, and the highlight of my high school experience was being selected as a cheerleader. The advantage of being a part of an ethnic minority school population exposed me to socializing and engaging with a very diverse student body.

At 16, I graduated with honors and was one of the class valedictorians. I won the graduating class award for "versatility," which, looking back, was oddly appropriate.

Surprisingly, my mother showed up at my high school graduation and immediately let me know that, with my freshly minted high school diploma, I would now be expected to find a job and would no longer receive any financial support, even though I was only 16.

I was not surprised by this declaration and was already accustomed to my independent lifestyle, though I would have to become financially independent as well. I felt a sense of freedom and relief because I was now master of my own destiny. And I knew my destiny depended on a college education.

My San Francisco experience gave me the strength to realize I could survive on my own. Facing an awkward home life in

Oakland taught me how to mask my loneliness by putting on a positive, confident, happy-go-lucky face so people would see me as "normal." I had found a way to define myself instead of letting the world define me.

Learning how to find a connection with people of all cultures and backgrounds provided me with a social safety net at a crucial time, as I navigated through adolescence on my own. My involvement with student activities helped me gain the recognition and approbation that fed my hunger for acceptance. This incessant drive for approval pushed me to constantly seek ways to prove my self-worth, beyond my teenage years and well into adulthood.

···

During my final year in high school my mother left Uncle Ed and suddenly moved to New York City. Even so, Uncle Ed continued to support me through my last year in high school. When I applied to colleges, I immediately realized I would not be able to qualify for a scholarship or financial aid because my family's income came from illegal gambling.

Determined to become financially independent at 16, I drew up a budget based on expenses I needed for tuition, books, food, housing, clothing, and transportation.

After researching my options, I chose San Francisco State University as the most practical alternative. The tuition was under $50 a semester. I was also able to rent a room at my old home, Mama's house in the Richmond district. Mama had retired from childcare and was now renting out rooms for extra income. San Francisco had an excellent public transit system, which meant I did not need a car.

Uncle Ed offered to pay part of my college education. I was touched by his generosity but declined his offer because he had already done so much to support me over the last four years. I did accept some seed money to help me get started during my first year, and he insisted that he at least pay for my room rental of $28 per month. To this day I remain indebted to this man's kindness and generosity, and for providing me with some semblance of a financial safety net.

During my first year at S.F. State, I took whatever jobs I could find, including cleaning houses, which I quickly realized was not my strength. Luckily, during my first semester, I was able to find a job at the college library shelving books for $1 an hour, which allowed me to work 20-30 hours a week between classes and still carry a full 16-unit class load.

When summer approached, the library offered me a full-time job typing catalog cards. This led to a job in the catalog department during the school year. Now I was earning hourly wages as a typist with full-time summer work; I could finance my college education on my own. Even with a demanding academic and work schedule, I had time to enjoy a full social life with a new group of college friends who lived in the City—the late Carole Ng, Vickie Kwan Woo and Emily Lee Chong. They taught me the ways of big city life—makeup, hair style, and dress. They also introduced me to new San Francisco friends and local haunts. We remain the best of friends and cherish our reunions.

I started dating Willie Seto, who was among a group of Sacramento boys I met at a high school dance in Oakland. We became reacquainted when he was in the Army stationed at the San Francisco Presidio just blocks away from Mama's house. What started as a date of convenience turned into a romance. When Willie was scheduled to ship out to Korea for two years, we decided to get engaged. I was 18, he was 21. During Willie's time in Korea, his Sacramento friends at UC Berkeley, Ken and Tommy Fat, Ed Jue, and Kellogg Chan, all helped to watch over me and included me in their social activities through the rest of my college years.

There was a comforting normalcy to college life—a contrast to my earlier years of tension and upheaval. The academics, the friendships, the job, and my social life reassured me that I was okay and could make my own way in the world.

I graduated in 1962 with a BA degree in Social Welfare and a minor in Psychology. I continued to work in the library as I waited to qualify, at 21, for my social welfare license. I looked forward to a profession where I would be able to help people in need, as I had been helped during my times of need.

Getting through college on my own boosted my self-confidence. During my younger years, I was forced to become emotionally independent, relying on my social skills for survival. The college experience showed me I also had the ability to be financially independent. Now that I was a college graduate with a degree, and engaged to be married, I was excited about the future.

Little did I know that destiny had a different path in mind for me.

With mother in S.F. Chinatown; My 3rd grade class at Jean Parker School

LOSS

"Dads hold our hands for a little while and hold our hearts forever."
—Anonymous

I cannot recall ever seeing my mother and father together except in some pictures of them holding me as an infant. My mother left about a year after I was born to sing in the gambling dens in Seattle. So, it was primarily my dad who visited me during the first years of my life.

As far as I can remember, whenever my dad came to Mama's house it was with some young, beautiful Chinese woman I automatically called Auntie. I had many "aunties." I learned years later that my father had broken my mother's heart with his philandering, and that was why she had left.

As a famous comedian in the Cantonese opera world, my father was a popular celebrity in Chinatown, known for his sense of humor, who loved to make people laugh on and off stage. I was told my father was a big fan of Charlie Chaplin and imitated Chaplin's moves and facial expressions, so they nicknamed him the Chinese Charlie Chaplin. I remembered him as a loving, soft spoken, chubby figure. People tell me he was gentle, with a heart of gold and a mischievous, fun-loving personality.

During our visits to Chinatown, he always attracted a crowd. Restaurant owners begged him to come in for a meal and merchants came out of their stores with gifts of food and toys for me. I loved the attention. It was so exciting being with my father because I knew he was someone special, and that made me feel special too. I also noticed he never snubbed fans who approached him on the street. He always took time to chat as I waited patiently, holding his hand.

My dad barely spoke English and, during my years at Mama's house, I only spoke English and some French Basque. So, my father and I became proficient in our own kind of sign language. He made me laugh all the time; we didn't need words to communicate the love we felt for each other. Then one day when I was about five years old, I recall seeing my father crying. He tried to explain in his broken English that he was returning to Hong Kong to pursue his increasingly successful theatrical career. He would not be seeing me for a long time.

A huge crowd came out the day my father went down to the San Francisco waterfront to board a ship bound for Hong Kong. I stood among his fans and watched him leave. It was the last time I saw my father.

...

After he left, I knew of my father only through his movies that were shown in San Francisco's Chinese theatres. In Hong Kong, as the premier Cantonese Opera comedian, his fame soared.

Later, I learned that the Chinese American woman I knew as Auntie Claire, one of his San Francisco paramours, had followed him to Hong Kong, where they married and had four children.

My father's life ended sadly and tragically. During an opera tour on the Chinese mainland, in Canton, the communist regime sealed the border between Hong Kong and China before my father was able to return. During the rise of the Cultural Revolution, my father was imprisoned along with others who represented the "elite society," including many from the art world and academia. Later I was told he was among those tortured, paraded through the streets, and stoned. He was charged with being pro-American and anti-revolutionary because he was caught talking about missing "the old world." He was condemned as a "monster and freak" and kept in a hard labor camp in rural China.

My half-sister, Julianne Look, who was 12 when my father died, told me the last time she saw him he was thin and frail and suffered from hypertension. His last words to his family were, "I feel very cold here. Bring me a quilt next time you come." Shortly thereafter, his body was found next to the toilets he was cleaning. It's not known whether he committed suicide or died from ill health. He was 54.

In 1968, I was working at the Honolulu International Airport when I learned of my father's death from two famous Hong Kong actresses, Yum Gim Fay and Bok Sheut Sin, who were passing through Hawaii on their way back to Hong Kong. One of my father's fellow actors, Lee Kok Sing, whom I called Uncle Lee, had settled in Honolulu to become a cook and restaurant owner. He arranged for them to meet me. They showed me a Chinese newspaper article about my father's passing and said he died from the effects of punishing hard labor.

My father's family in China returned to the U.S. because Auntie Claire was a U.S. citizen. They live in the Bay Area now and only in recent years have we gotten to know each other. My stepsister Julianne stays in touch and shares wonderful memories of my father. I remain grateful to my Auntie Claire for her devotion to my father, and it brings me joy to see his resemblance in my half-brothers and -sisters.

My experience with my father was brief, but his impact on my life loomed large. He made me feel special as the daughter of a celebrity. I saw the power of his magnetic personality and sense of humor, how friends and fans loved being near him. My father's kindness and the way he paid attention to every fan who stopped him on the street left a lasting impression on me. He made me feel that I belonged to someone, and it was a long time after his death before I was able to feel that way again.

...

"Forgiveness is not about forgetting, it is about letting go."
—William P. Young

I never had what I would call a real mother-daughter relationship. We came from different worlds. My mother was known among her friends as direct, opinionated, and temperamental. She cut a glamourous figure with style, charm, and an engaging sense of humor. People tended to forgive her bossy behavior. Sometimes she would embarrass me in public with inappropriate comments or humor. She had no filter.

My first husband, Willie Seto, and I eloped to Carmel. I had just turned 21. My mother didn't attend the wedding. Later, my mother was living in New York when I married my current husband, Ron Tom, but she happened to be in San Francisco at the time of our wedding in Sacramento and she called to say she wanted to attend. She told me she wanted to make sure I made the right choice this time. Much to my surprise, she participated in the traditional Chinese wedding tea ceremony gifting me with some of her most exquisite pieces of Chinese jewelry and fur coats. I also think she was trying to impress Ron's parents, Wayne and Mabel Tom, who were very well known among the prominent Chinese business families in Sacramento.

After our daughter, Stephanie, was born and old enough to travel at a year and a half, Ron and I took her to New York to see my mother. As I watched her holding Stephanie, I realized it was the first time I ever saw her act in any way maternal. She was so excited she could not wait to show off her granddaughter to friends in her Chinatown neighborhood on Manhattan's lower eastside.

Of course, my mother had an ulterior motive.

After a 30-minute walk around the neighborhood, Stephanie had amassed over 3,000 dollars in cash from my mother's gambler friends, who abided by the Chinese tradition of offering good luck money to babies seen for the first time.

...

My mother was working in a Chinatown gambling den and her boyfriend, Benny Ong, was the chief syndicate boss in New York Chinatown. During our visit, Uncle Benny gave us unlimited cash to spend, for a personal driver to take us shopping, to dine at the best restaurants, and to get the best tickets to the Broadway shows. Money was no object.

Every night, some bigshot friend of Benny's would host a ten course Chinese banquet for us, a show of respect in Chinatown. I had never seen my mother happier. When Uncle Benny asked Ron what type of car he liked, Ron's response was, "A Porsche." Uncle Benny promised he would get him one when we returned to California.

One evening as Uncle Benny was doing his rounds of the underground gambling dens, he asked Ron to come along. Ron, who grew up in a Chinese American working-class family, was fascinated by my mother's exotic, dangerous world. He felt it was like being in the movies as he walked through secret alleyways with beefy bodyguards guarding dimly lit rooms where men at small tables played a game with a bowl of buttons that are tossed on a table of squares and counted out in fours. Most were laborers and restaurant workers around Chinatown. There was a cook who prepared food for the players, and a bar.

Uncle Benny would collect bags of cash as he visited each den. When Ron asked if Benny was afraid to carry so much cash out in the streets of Chinatown, Uncle Benny looked at Ron and said, "No one will dare touch me in these streets."

Two weeks after our return to California, as Ron was busy selecting the color of his new Porsche, Uncle Benny made headlines in the New York papers.

His arrest for tax evasion was a major coup for law enforcement because Uncle Benny was considered the head of the most powerful Tong association in New York. He became an underground hero because he refused to testify against the Mafia bosses who controlled gambling in New York's Chinatown and Little Italy. As a result, he served a long prison term for tax evasion. I'm told he was well treated inside the prison walls.

My mother's meager earnings at the dens were no longer sufficient to support her daily needs and gambling addiction. She even turned her apartment into a Mahjong room where she would host high- stakes gambling parties and cook for the players. She was paid a small cut of the winnings and Ron and I sent her monthly checks to help with basic living expenses. However, she would frequently ask for extra money for household repairs, travel to Hong Kong to see a sick family friend, or for expensive medical and dental bills. She also asked me to return the jewelry and furs she gave me for my wedding, which I knew she would use to repay gambling debts.

As her requests became larger and more frequent, we decided to visit her in New York to check on her living conditions and health. One morning while my mother slept, Ron stormed out of the bathroom. "Remember all the money we've been sending your mother for dental work these past years?" He showed me a glass of water with her upper and lower dentures. I didn't know whether to laugh or cry. My mother was not happy when Ron advised her that, from now on, we would not pay for extra expenses unless she provided receipts.

From that point on, my husband, whom my mother used to call "her handsome movie star son-in-law," suddenly became "that cheap SOB." There was no love lost between them after that. Ron tried his best to be kind and generous to my mother because he respected the fact that, as her only child, I had a duty to take care of her. He never complained. But he never got over resenting her for the way she treated me during my years growing up.

· · ·

A heavy chain smoker, my mother was diagnosed with lung cancer in 1991. She was 74.

I flew to New York to be by her side as she was being checked into the hospital. When I saw her small, frail body, an unfamiliar sense of compassion and attachment rushed through me. Perhaps it was the frightened look on her face, bewildered by what was happening to her, that made me realize for the first time that she really needed me.

Ron, Stephanie, and I visited her together one last time a few months later. She was growing weaker from the cancer that by now had metastasized throughout her body. I commuted back and forth to New York on the redeye because I had just started a new job as the chief of staff to President Pro Tem of the California Senate, David Roberti. I was fortunate that my dear friend, Joyce Yuen, daughter of Chinese movie star, Suey Yin Fay, was in New York and took great care of my mother during my absence.

The doctor wanted my mother to start radiation treatments, but she resisted stubbornly, insisting she had tuberculosis. Ron and I seriously considered putting her in a hospital in Sacramento to be closer to us but my mother, weak as she was, insisted she would never stay in Sacramento because it was too boring, and the Mahjong players in Sacramento were only small-time gamblers.

As the weeks passed, I knew my mother's health was failing rapidly. One night I was lying next to her in her hospital bed. The nurses knew of my West Coast commute and allowed me to stay beyond the normal visiting hours. When I told my mom that I was flying home the next day but would be back in a couple of days, it triggered a fierce temper tantrum. She accused me of being a neglectful daughter who was more concerned about her job than her mother. Then she started comparing me to the daughters of her other friends.

I could not believe I was hearing this woman, who was missing for most of my life, accusing me of being a negligent daughter, compounded by the fact that Ron and I had been supporting her financially for the past decade, with no hint of gratitude. This was the straw that broke the camel's back.

Luckily, we were in a single room—because I jumped off the bed and started to cry, screaming at her and releasing all the pain, rejection, and anger I had repressed my entire life. I asked her in my broken Chinese, "How dare you accuse me of being a negligent daughter when you never had the decency to ever inconvenience yourself to be a mother to me?" I didn't hesitate to angrily remind her of the abuse I suffered in Chinatown, only to have her turn her back on me. Or the years I had spent taking care of myself because she did not want to be a mother. I simply told her that she did not have the right to call herself my mother, period.

I am not sure how long I went on with my outburst.

But I remember she lay expressionless and silent on the bed as I screamed at her, as if she was listening to me for the first time. After a moment of awkward silence, with me sobbing uncontrollably, she said in Chinese, with a deadpan face, "Well, at least I see you inherited my temper." That totally stopped me, and I burst out laughing because at that moment I realized for better or worse, this was my mother; this was simply who she was.

That release of my lifelong repressed anger and emotion toward my mother freed me to finally be able to love her for who she was. I climbed back on the bed with her, laughing and crying at the same time, to cherish that rare moment of us holding on to each other as mother and daughter. I whispered to her, "I love you mom." This was the first time I saw my mom cry.

I only wish she had said the words, "I love you, too."

...

When I called Ron to tell him about the incident that night, he said, wisely, "You're lucky that you had the chance to reveal to your mother all the pent-up emotions you've repressed all your life—because this frees you to let go of that resentment while she's still alive."

When I returned to California, I called to let her know my schedule of return, but I could not find her. I panicked because she was supposed to start her radiation treatments. I was told that she took a trip to the horse races with her oxygen tank in tow. She died two days later. I know she did not want to endure radiation and chemotherapy treatments, and my mother never did anything she did not want to do. She died within four months of her diagnosis.

Ron and I went to New York to arrange for the funeral. I did not know much about my mother's life in New York but was startled at how few people showed up for her service.

We abided by my mother's wishes to have a traditional funeral with a parade around her apartment. This meant hiring professional mourners, a band, and a minimum of three limousines, because one limousine is considered disrespectful and even numbers are unlucky.

My mother's funeral was small, and soon most of the people had to return to work. I had to beg five people to stay and ride in the limousines.

Several people at the funeral apparently had come to ask me to pay off my mother's gambling debts. Luckily, Ron took over, telling them that in accordance with American culture and law, I was not responsible for my mother's debts. The word must have gotten around Chinatown fast because by the time we got back to her apartment after the parade and funeral dinner, my mother's apartment had been looted of furniture and personal belongings, apparently as repayment of her gambling debts.

Since I had to fly directly from New York to Washington D.C. for my first Senate legislative trip with Senate President Pro Tem David Roberti, I asked Ron to take my mother's ashes home with him. Ron suggested we send my mother's ashes to Sacramento via UPS. I wasn't sure if he was kidding, but in the end, he put the container with my mother's ashes in a Montebello racetrack bag and carried the tote home on the plane.

While going through airport security, the agent asked Ron what was in the tote bag.

"My mother-in-law," Ron said, not missing a beat.

When the agent opened the cardboard box, he was terrified. "Oh my god, it's his mama in here." When it came to my mother, nothing was normal. With Ron, I think she had the last laugh.

Today my mother's ashes lie in the East Lawn cemetery in Sacramento where I can be near her to make up for all the time we spent apart. To deal with my grief, I later wrote about my mother in one of my *Asian Week* Capitol Watch columns. It was one of the most-read columns I ever wrote.

...

There are many mother/daughter stories that help define who we are today, for better or worse.

While my mother lacked maternal instincts, as far as she was concerned, she fulfilled her responsibilities by providing financial support until I graduated from high school. As I look back, being independent by the time I was 14 was key to my being able to become self-reliant without ever doubting I was going to "make it." While many of my peers were still dealing with parental expectations, I was living the life of self-determination. I consider that an invaluable gift my mother gave me.

陸雲飛領金牌時所影

評雪辨蹤

Father receiving a monetary award from the San Francisco fans; Father in a character role in the Cantonese Opera; Last family gathering with mother in New York

BOOK TWO

Climbing the ladder...

"If someone offers you an amazing opportunity and you are unsure you can do it, say yes, then learn how to do it later."
—Richard Branson

THE FIRST RUNG

After graduating from college, I moved to Sacramento with my first husband, Willie Seto, who was starting a career in retail as an assistant manager of the K Street Woolworth Company.

My first professional position was at Sacramento State University where I was offered an opportunity to serve as an assistant to the college personnel officer, the late John Samara. Samara was known as one of the toughest, yet most highly regarded college personnel officers in the California State University system. While this position was not in my desired field of social welfare, helping people looking for jobs appealed to me.

Samara knew that, at 21, I was a novice in the field of personnel management and he generously took me under his wing to teach me the basics of the job. I tried to absorb as much as I could in the two years I was in this job, and Samara delegated more and more responsibilities to me with the hope of promoting me to a management position.

But after two years, my husband was transferred to Honolulu to become the assistant manager of the Waikiki Woolworth store. It was not easy to leave Sac State and Samara, who became more like a mentor than a boss to me. As I was leaving, I recall him telling me that my "people- and problem-solving skills" would be great assets in helping me to succeed in whatever career path I chose. However, Samara cautioned that, as I climbed the management ladder, "It's more important to be respected for one's integrity and fairness than it is to be liked." He already sensed that one of my weaknesses was a need to be liked and accepted by everyone, and he was right. It took me decades to overcome this.

Moving to the glamorous Hawaiian Islands with Willie was exciting to me.

After my brief stint as a personnel assistant with Liberty House, Hawaii's high-end retail department store (which was later bought out by Macy's), I landed a personnel management position with Host International, Inc., at the Honolulu International Airport.

This company managed all the food service, catering, restaurants and gift concessions at the airport. Host International was the only non-union shop at the airport and it was constantly under the threat of organizing drives by food service employees. The general manager, George Piquette, was looking for someone who would not only manage their personnel program but also help convince workers that they did not need a union to negotiate for better working conditions and benefits.

Having zero experience in labor relations and overseeing 200 employees—generations of locally born Asian Pacific Islanders working as waitresses, bartenders, cooks, kitchen staff, salesclerks and maintenance personnel—was a major challenge for this 23-year-old, who had never managed before.

Even though I was Asian American, I spoke with a mainland accent and was new to the Hawaiian culture and lifestyle. As far as these workers were concerned, I was someone management had brought in from the outside.

I was fortunate to bond with the two locally born Asian American women in the office, Bea Iwata, the account manager, and Jane Kawakami, Piquette's executive assistant. Both were popular with rank and file employees and served as their channel to the "big bosses" in the executive offices. I asked them to introduce me to each and every Host employee so I would be able to identify them all by name. I made a point of daily morning rounds so the employees would become familiar with me and my interest in their jobs.

I gained instant credibility when I noticed the employee lounge and restroom were so dirty and neglected that employees avoided them completely and instead used facilities elsewhere in the airport. I asked management for a small budget to refurbish and paint the lounge, which endeared me to the staff, who subsequently became more open and friendly. The more they saw me, the more comfortable they were to share stories about their families and, eventually, about their job situation.

As the employees started to trust me, I was able to address some of their issues with management and helped negotiate grievances some employees had with supervisors in a fair, open manner so there was no backlash to their complaints. I helped promote diversity among the supervisorial and management ranks by encouraging the executive office to consider rank-and-file employees who showed an interest and had leadership skills. I created a monthly newsletter to keep employees informed of company news and highlighted exceptional employees.

Host International's corporate office liked the newsletter so much that they started one in every airport facility they managed around the country.

I attribute my success at this job to Piquette's willingness to support my recommendations and my ability to gain the trust of the employees by simply being there and listening. Native Hawaiians thrive on the "aloha spirit" of friendship, family, and loyalty, and Host International cultivated this spirit by sponsoring annual company picnics and holiday parties for the employees and their families. The company offered competitive salaries and benefits that thwarted union organizing efforts, and Host remained the only non-union employer at the airport during my tenure there in the 1960s.

Unfortunately, the focus and demands of my professional career did not bode well for my first marriage. It wasn't Willie's fault; I was just too young at 21 to be married. We divorced after three years.

...

After four years with Host, I took a job as the public affairs director of Honolulu's Fort Street mall project which aimed to revitalize Honolulu's downtown.

Before I started, I took a quick trip to Sacramento to see my college friends.

I was single and enjoying that life in Hawaii—and even embarking on part-time singing gigs at clubs and military bases. But, my Sacramento friends, Lina Fat and Nanci Jan, had different ideas for me. They wanted to reunite me with another college friend, Ron Tom, who also had recently become single.

Lina and Nanci heard from their husbands, my old college buddies Ken Fat and Mike Jan, that Ron and I had enjoyed a brief fling when we met in Oakland at a dance. He was 18 and I was 15 at the time. I thought he was the most handsome 6'1" Chinese boy I'd ever laid eyes on—and can honestly say he was my first love. We danced all night together and ended up pen pals, but the distance between Sacramento and Oakland was too far for the brief romance to survive.

Now, with us both divorced and single again, we reconnected thanks to an elaborate romantic dinner party arranged by Lina and her husband Ken in Sacramento. Their scheme worked. I spent the rest of my vacation in Sacramento being wooed by Ron, who convinced me to return to Honolulu in time to stop the press release announcing my new job, pack my things, and return to Sacramento.

Ron and I married within six months of my return in January 1970.

I came back to Sacramento with a newfound confidence as a manager and executive.

I dreaded leaving Hawaii and the warm aloha spirit of the Hawaiian people, and I could not fathom what type of profession in Sacramento could possibly match the glamorous, exciting job I had in the Hawaii restaurant, hotel and tourist industry. But being able to marry my first love made the decision much easier.

WELCOME TO POLITICS

Returning to Sacramento to marry Ron, followed by the birth of our only child, Stephanie, a year later, led to one of the biggest changes in my life.

For the first time, I had a family of my own. It was a new sensation and it took me a while to adjust to being a stay-at-home mom, caring for an infant daughter. Financially independent since I was 16, I wasn't accustomed to someone supporting me. And because I'd never experienced a genuine mother-daughter relationship, I also had to learn about motherhood. Stephanie was the first human being who truly belonged to me and I instinctively wanted to give her everything I missed by not really having a mother of my own.

By 1974, with my daughter entering pre-school, I was ready to rejoin the job market. Our next-door neighbor, David Kim, a lobbyist, and his wife, Sarah Reyes Kim, both worked in and around the state Legislature. David suggested that I interview for a part-time job with the new Assembly majority whip, Joe Montoya, who was looking for an Asian American to serve as a legislative assistant because Montoya represented a heavily Asian district, Monterey Park in East Los Angeles.

Being totally apolitical, I had never been inside the state Capitol until I arrived for my interview with the assemblyman and his chief of staff, Bobby Garcia. I was so surprised that Garcia was so young; but he was extremely impressive, quizzing me about my background. I could tell he was checking my demeanor and personality to determine if I had the confidence, skills, and enthusiasm to succeed in this position.

The assemblyman himself was equally warm and friendly. I made it a point to say that I had no political experience but was not afraid of the challenge of learning new things, adding, with a smile, that I was a quick learner.

Bobby was encouraging when he remarked, "No one can determine if you can succeed in the state Capitol, because of the political nature of the institution. It doesn't matter how much political experience you have: you either get it or you don't."

Soon after my interview, I received a call from Bobby telling me I got the job. I could not believe my luck, that with no political experience I was going to work at the state Capitol. Little did I know, the key to getting jobs in the Capitol is more about who you know, not what you know. Thanks to David Kim, I got a break.

I was totally enamored with my new career. I did not even think about job security; I was too excited learning how the legislative and political process worked. I was awed by the amazing power and influence one had just being associated with the state Legislature. I could not get over the fact that decisions made in the Capitol impacted the lives of every Californian. Even back then, California's cutting-edge leadership made it the number one state in the U.S., thus the saying, "As goes California, so goes the nation."

The work environment in the Capitol was dominated by highly intelligent, energetic personalities whose decisions and behavior were constantly under public scrutiny. I also noticed the obvious: it was dominated by white, male legislators and staff with minimal diversity. I wondered about the chances of a minority woman like me succeeding there with no experience.

There were very few women serving in professional positions, with the majority working as support staff. Many who held clerical positions had college degrees, but still jumped at the opportunity to get a foot in the door with hopes of advancing into professional jobs. I was one of the lucky ones to start out as a professional staffer, even though my position was on the "lowly" side.

With no formal training program, I was on my own to sink or swim. It turned out to be a good test of my ability to work in an environment driven by a Darwinian, survival-of-the-fittest mentality.

In addition to Montoya's staff, I was most fortunate to have some other key mentors who took me under their wings and helped me grasp the complex power structure and political dynamics of the legislature.

My first mentor was David Townsend, chief of staff to state Senator Bob Presley, whose office was adjacent to Montoya's. David was (and remains) a savvy political consultant whose campaign experience with some of the state's most prominent legislators, such as Sen. George Zenovich and Speaker Bob Moretti, made him one of the elite staffers in the Capitol. Coming from a family of adopted siblings from different ethnic backgrounds, David was delighted to see an Asian face among the professionals in the building and took it upon himself to introduce me to the major players. He cleared away many barriers I would have faced if I had been forced to navigate the who's who in the Capitol on my own. David eventually became my go-to person whenever I had questions about the process or personalities I had to endure as a novice in this ego-driven workplace.

One of my greatest assets throughout my Capitol experience, and maybe to this day, was my willingness to acknowledge what I didn't know, and then boldly approach someone with the expertise to educate me. I soon found out that most people are willing to help—if we're only willing to ask.

Montoya's legislative secretary, Rachel Fontes, was another godsend who taught me the basics of the legislative process, including understanding its particular vocabulary, reading the publications, and understanding how to work with Assemblyman Montoya. She taught me early in the game to respect the legislative secretaries who often served as gatekeepers to members.

And then I met my first personal "buddy," a petite Asian-American woman, Georgette Imura, a few years younger than I, who started her career right after high school. A Sacramento native, she married her high school sweetheart, Roy, and had one son, Todd, and was pregnant with her second son, Aaron, when I met her. At this time, Georgette was a seasoned legislative professional who started as a secretary to the late Sacramento Assemblyman Leroy Green. She worked her way up the ladder to become the legislative assistant to the Assembly majority caucus chair, the late Julian Dixon. Georgette was so excited to meet another Asian-American woman legislative assistant in the Capitol she immediately embraced me when we met.

During those days you could count the total number of Asian American professionals in the state Capitol with two hands. From that day forward we were like two peas in a pod, now for more than 45 years.

. . .

Every legislative assistant is given a package of bills to manage. I became obsessed with my bill assignments, thinking it was incumbent on me to make sure they all succeeded through the legislative process. But I learned my first lesson in politics the hard way.

My first legislation was a consumer bill on truthful labeling of fat content in ground beef packaging. It sailed through the Assembly. To ensure passage in the Senate, I did everything I could to neutralize the opposition of the Grocer's Association and the beef industry, and personally polled the Senate policy committee members, which allowed me to assure Montoya that the bill would pass with a one-vote margin.

But during the committee hearing a Senator did a last-minute flip, dooming it to failure. I was devastated.

After the committee hearing, I rushed back to my office because I didn't want Montoya and Bobby to see me break into tears. I felt responsible for failing Montoya. He and Bobby followed me to my small supply closet office barely able to restrain their laughter as they told me if I was going to take a loss of every bill this hard, I would never be able to survive in the Capitol.

They explained that this specific senator flipped his vote at the last minute because Montoya had just filed to run against him for his senate seat and his no vote had nothing to do with the merits of the bill and everything to do with his not wanting Montoya to achieve any legislative success. Welcome to politics. (As it turned out, Montoya did challenge this senator in the next election—and beat him.) As for the bill, it passed the second time during reconsideration.

Today, when I buy ground beef and see the fat designation on the regular, lean, and extra-lean package labels, I smile because this was my first bill, signed into law by Governor Jerry Brown during his first term as governor.

. . .

During my second year with Montoya, the staff was enjoying a Christmas holiday lunch when Montoya received a call from Speaker Leo McCarthy, informing Montoya that McCarthy's former chief of staff, newly elected Assemblyman Art Agnos, was taking over the majority whip position. Suddenly, all of us on the majority whip payroll were out of jobs.

In this moment, I realized what the term "serving at the pleasure of…" meant for Capitol staff. Legislative staff positions are exempt from civil service. I had never experienced being laid off with a 30-day notice.

By this time, I was hooked on working at the Capitol, working with influential decision makers and enjoying the addicting power by association. I had finally found a job I loved, and *I did not want to leave.*

Montoya and his staff were like family. Nonetheless, I now had to hustle to find a job with another elected member. (Sadly, some years after I left his office, Montoya was convicted of extortion, though five of the seven convictions were ultimately dismissed.)

During this time, Chief Administrative Officer (CAO) of the Assembly Fred Taugher was seeking a deputy administrative officer to handle personnel. Taugher was under pressure to hire an ethnic minority because the minority legislative caucuses and Speaker McCarthy were demanding that the professional legislative staff diversify to better reflect the demographics of the state. It was no secret that during those years, in the early 70s, the composition of the Capitol staff and elected officials was predominantly white males.

I nailed my interview with Taugher—and, being an ethnic minority female with a personnel management background, I was a top contender for the job. However, the Assembly Rules Committee Chairman, Lou Papan, would have to approve this appointment, and I was warned that he was being heavily lobbied by Black Caucus legislators to select an African American male candidate who had no personnel experience.

I was terrified to meet Papan, a heavy-set former FBI agent with the nickname "The Enforcer," who had an intimidating reputation around the Capitol for his unpredictable temper and unabashed ability to bully people. I was hoping my cheerful, confident demeanor would win over this intimidating Rules Committee chairman.

But when I walked into Papan's office for my interview, he did not greet me or make eye contact. He simply asked why I wanted the job. After I told him of my personnel management and legislative experience, he asked what my husband did for a living. I told him Ron was a pharmacist.

Papan then asked me why I wasn't supporting my husband's business by helping at the cosmetic counter (he had assumed that Ron owned a drugstore). I was so flabbergasted by the question that I said in a whisper that my husband worked for a chain-store pharmacy. Here I was being treated in a sexist manner, but I was so intimidated that I could not respond intelligently.

I don't even remember how the interview ended because I was so shaken by the question. I could not wait to get out of his office.

Seeing how distressed I was, Fred Taugher suggested I ask some legislators to talk to Papan on my behalf. I turned to March Fong Eu and Assemblyman Vic Fazio, who later joined Congress, for help.

I recall Fazio telling me in disbelief that when Papan found out I drove a Mercedes, he felt the job should go to a male family provider who needed the money more than a woman from a dual income household who drove a Mercedes and whose husband drove a Porsche.

Ironically, it was Georgette's boss, Julian Dixon, chair of the Black Caucus, who was pushing the African American male candidate for the job. He told Georgette, who was advocating on my behalf, why Papan would not be selecting me, to which the feisty Georgette retorted sarcastically, "Oh, that's a great reason to disqualify an experienced candidate, because she happens to drive a Mercedes."

I knew that I had a compelling case for a job discrimination suit if I were turned down, but it also would have ended my Capitol career. Also, the "Asian" in me did not want to create waves that would be noticed in the Capitol's good-old-boy network, so I was prepared to just move on.

To my surprise, I got the job.

Taugher offered no explanation as to why Papan had a change of heart. But I surmised that Taugher ultimately went over Papan's head and spoke directly to Speaker McCarthy. Fortunately, Taugher and Papan had a positive, long-term working relationship, which allowed Papan to defer to his colleague's desire for me to get the job.

My appointment was a politically sensitive decision for Speaker McCarthy because he had to go against the wishes of the Black Caucus members who had backed him for the speakership. But McCarthy's reputation for integrity and his willingness to stand up for what is right, over political expediency, had prevailed.

Even though I got the job, I was not proud of how I'd handled my interview with Papan. I did not have the courage to do what so many women role models do today, to stand up for themselves, no matter the consequences. I took the easy way out by staying silent. Luckily, I had the chance to redeem myself later by helping other women learn not to make the same mistake I made.

...

My first challenge was gaining the trust of a hostile boss.

When I started my new job, Papan did not invite me to meetings to discuss personnel issues. When Taugher was persistent to include me, Papan would ignore my presence. He gradually got used to my being in the room, and Taugher would direct me to speak up so that Papan eventually talked to me directly.

After my first year on the job, Papan was still cool toward me. I needed to gain his trust by proving that I could also be of value to him beyond my responsibilities to the Rules Committee.

Papan's district included San Mateo and Daly City, which had a high percentage of Asian/Filipino voters. I knew that my activism within the communities of Asian & Pacific Islander Americans (APIA) would be helpful in his district, so I volunteered to become his eyes and ears with these constituents. I was able to strengthen his relationship with APIA leaders in his district, who included my dear friend, Alice Bulos, a revered leader of local Filipino Democrats.

Filipino-Americans were often lost in the political shadows of the more dominant Chinese, Japanese, and Korean American activists. Alice inserted herself into all the Democratic Asian American activities as a constant reminder of the Filipino American constituency. As a result of her leadership in encouraging her community to become more politically involved, she became known as the godmother of Filipino American democrats and was revered by all politicians who wanted the support of the Filipino American democratic voter base in California. I was finally able to gain Papan's trust and became an integral part of his Capitol and district staff family which, at that time, included Mike Thompson, who now serves in Congress, and Assemblyman Ken Cooley, the current chair of the Assembly Rules Committee.

Serving in my new capacity as the personnel director of the Assembly meant that I now served all 80 members instead of just one legislator. I was so eager to make a good first impression that I would ask Taugher, who had a decade of experience as the Assembly CAO, to brief me on the different personalities and quirks of each legislator I would be meeting for the first time.

Each legislator had a unique intellect and demeanor, as well as personality traits ranging from gracious, shy, soft spoken, gregarious, receptive, warm, friendly, and humble, to demanding, sexist, aloof, egotistical, cocky, demeaning, patronizing, temperamental, and racist.

I researched the background of legislators, the composition of their districts, and their personal relationships with other members to help me find a positive way to connect at our first meetings. This proved successful most of the time and helped me survive some unpleasant encounters as well. I learned which legislators were safe to befriend and which I should hold at arm's length. I found I could disarm some of the most difficult legislators with my sense of humor or a directness that they were unaccustomed to hearing from staff, and even more so from an Asian woman.

The late Assemblyman John Vasconcellos, for example, was as temperamental as he was brilliant and wielded great influence as the powerful Ways and Means chair. He also became a mentor to me. He was so sensitive to the barriers I faced as a minority woman that we formed an immediate friendship that lasted beyond his years as a legislator.

Vasconcellos's seniority and influence in the Capitol was further enhanced by his close relationship to Speaker Willie Brown. Vasconcellos was in the habit of always wanting to hire more staff, even though he already had the largest staff in the Capitol. He would routinely threaten to resign if Brown disapproved his requests. The Speaker was aware of my very close relationship with Vasconcellos and happily delegated these conversations to me to handle with Vasconcellos directly.

When I had to deny one of Vasconcellos's frequent requests for additional personnel, I went to his office with a notebook and pen and gave it to him before we started the discussion.

He said, "What's this for?"

I said, "You'll need it for your handwritten resignation when I tell you that we cannot authorize your latest personnel request."

John did not exactly laugh, but he got the picture. Whenever we had these discussions, after John got over his anger with me, he would calmly ask, "How are you doing, are they treating you ok?" It's one of the reasons why I adored this man.

It's amazing what a smile and a positive, confident demeanor, along with a quick sense of humor, can do. But I also had my share of ugly incidents with members who would resort to racist name-calling, calling me "slant-eye bitch" or "dragon lady" to my face (and worse, behind my back).

Some just bluntly told me they didn't need to deal with me and would take their matter to the CAO, Papan, or the Speaker. Some legislators succeeded with this approach, but not on a regular basis. More often than not, the CAO and Papan backed me up. Understanding the political nature of the Capitol, I would often confer with the CAO and Papan before I embarked on any sensitive personnel discussions with legislators, to make sure I wasn't overstepping my authority, understanding I was primarily the messenger for the CAO, Rules chair, or Speaker.

I refused to let legislators see how their disparaging behavior affected me. After these incidents, some would apologize, while others were visibly embarrassed to face me afterwards. But I continued to maintain a professional relationship with them, with no change in my demeanor. I did not want to confront those who made racist or sexist slurs, nor did I discuss these incidences with the CAO, Papan, or the Speaker. I had nothing to gain and everything to lose. I felt it was simply my cross to bear as a minority woman.

Gov. Jerry Brown and former Assemblymen Joe Montoya at signing of hamburger label bill; Assembly Rules Chair Lou Papan

CREDIBILITY AND STRUGGLE

I developed my own network of support, especially among the African American women legislators (Maxine Waters, Gwen Moore, Teresa Hughes, and Diane Watson) and Assemblyman Art Torres, who became a lifelong mentor to me in my personal and professional life. I even had close relationships with Republican leaders such as Assemblymen Pat Nolan, the late Bill Lancaster and the late Senator Ken Maddy, who took me under their wings and vouched for me whenever a Republican accused me of playing partisan politics with their personnel requests.

After years of working hard to gain credibility in my deputy role, I was able to acquire the respect of the majority of legislators, Democrats and Republicans alike, who saw me trying my best to help resolve their staff personnel issues within the Assembly Rules guidelines and trusted my word when I had to simply say, "It can't be done."

Some were especially appreciative of my willingness to warn them about personnel practices in their offices that would raise red flags under public scrutiny. They also trusted that I would not betray their confidences.

I was also gaining public recognition for my role in the legislature, featured among the Best and Brightest in Sacramento

Magazine, touted as one of the most influential legislative staffers by the California Journal, and featured in a story about my position in the state Capitol in the Sunday *Sacramento Bee.*

One of my proudest achievements as the personnel officer of the Assembly was when Speaker McCarthy and his chief of staff, the late Bob Toigo, wanted to diversify the Assembly's professional staff to better reflect the demographics of California. There was no applicants' pool of ethnically diverse candidates because the classic way to get a position in the Capitol was through personal relationships. Toigo's concept was for me to aggressively work with the ethnic minority legislative caucuses, professional organizations, and college campuses to recruit the best and brightest women and a pool of ethnic minority policy consultants to work for the Assembly.

Within two years, Bob and I were able to triple the number of professional women and ethnic minority professionals in the Capitol.

California's legislature was the first to conduct such an aggressive diversity outreach program in the 1970s. This program was so unique that the National Conference of State Legislatures asked us to conduct a workshop at their national conference to introduce this program to other states with a large diverse population. Once again, California's legislature was on the cutting edge of change—and Speaker McCarthy was the first to recognize the value of having a diverse team of policy experts guiding California's policies.

Another factor that helped empower me in my role was that Papan was feared by so many legislators that they preferred to deal with me on day-to-day personnel issues, rather than deal with the unpredictable Papan.

The longer I worked with Papan, the more I could predict his instincts and reactions to personnel issues. Papan's growing trust in my judgement gave me enormous influence in the Capitol and he, in turn, became my staunchest supporter and protector.

...

Handling the sexual harassment in the Capitol during this era was like being plopped into the Wild West.

In the 70s, there were no term limits for legislators and the women's rights movement was in its infancy. There were no Assembly personnel policies precluding legislators from having personal relationships with staff, and there was no real structure in place to deal with sexual harassment within the Capitol.

In fact, there were so many consensual relationships between legislators, staff, and lobbyists, that it was accepted as part of the norm within the Capitol world. Some legislators and staff even lived together when the legislators were in Sacramento during session.

Unfortunately, women who were victims of unwanted sexual advances simply preferred to quietly leave the Capitol for work elsewhere. In this male dominated work environment, legislators had the right to hire and fire at will, with no oversight or repercussions. And, worse, there was no incentive for legislators to adopt any internal grievance process to protect against employees' harassment. In short, women felt powerless in the existing Capitol environment.

It was rare for a woman to bring this type of behavior to my attention. When one would confide in me, I was sworn to secrecy, because she knew this type of allegation could result in her being blackballed from working for any other legislators. The good-old-boy network prevailed.

The only option I had available to protect the victim was to try to place her in another office as soon as possible. One time, I transferred a victim of sexual harassment to my own office to serve as my personal secretary—incurring the wrath of her former boss, who was furious that I "stole" his staff without his permission.

If there was a serious pattern of staff turnover amid sexual harassment rumors surrounding a specific legislator, I would bring it to the attention of the CAO or Papan, with the understanding that these types of problems were to be handled "member to member," which meant staff was not to get involved.

From time to time, I experienced momentary flirtatious behavior from a few of the legislators, but never to the point of harassment. Legislators were so accustomed to my sense of humor that I was able to "play off" their flirtations by looking the legislator in the eye and saying with a laugh, "You're not seriously going where I think you're going with this conversation, are you?" This tactic would invoke an embarrassed response such as, "You know I'm just kidding," which would allow me to smile and quickly return to the business at hand.

I also believe I was protected from harassment because I was in a position of authority and worked for a boss who was very protective of his staff. Papan comes from an old-fashioned Greek culture and he made it clear to everyone in the Capitol that his staff was family and he was the patriarch. Anyone who "messed" with his family would face the consequences.

The professional career opportunities and upward mobility for women in the Capitol during this era often relied on whom you knew. However, there was a growing number of some extraordinary professional women who were able to break into the legislature through the Assembly Fellowship program that provided opportunities for women to start in professional positions in the Assembly. Elizabeth Kersten, Barbara Moore and Leah Cartabruno were among this class of female consultants as well as the talented press secretary Bobbie Metzger.

I was one of the very few women in a position of executive authority in the sexually charged male-dominated culture of the Capitol. In this environment, people tended to assume that any woman in a senior management level position probably "slept her way up the ladder."

One day after I had just disciplined an employee for carrying a concealed weapon to work, the Rules executive secretary, Julie

Garcia (now Angelides) came into my office in tears telling me that there was a rumor around the Capitol that a sergeant caught me giving Papan a blow job in his office!

I didn't take it seriously and considered it a ridiculous rumor that was beyond belief. But I had entered the Capitol building that morning as a respected Deputy CAO and by the time I left the building, I was being called a slut.

For the next few days, I continued to put forward my best public face to demonstrate that the rumor did not affect me. But when a Dan Walters column in *The Sacramento Bee* repeated the rumor, though without naming the parties, I was devastated. I saw this as giving the rumor credibility. In the meantime, the Capitol was on alert because Papan was so furious that he was on the warpath to fire anyone suspected to have started this rumor. This only created a bigger furor.

When Speaker Willie Brown checked in to see how I was doing, he tried to cheer me up by saying, "People only get talked about if they are 'somebody,' so it goes with the territory." Somehow that didn't cheer me up. But he did say that Papan was not helping matters by overreacting. I felt totally helpless.

The next day I dropped in to see Assemblywoman Maxine Waters, who had a reputation as the toughest woman in the Assembly. She could see how upset I was and said, "What's up, baby?" which Maxine used as a term of endearment. This opened the floodgates of angry tears and humiliation. She took me in her arms and sternly looked at me and said, "Oh, no, I don't want to see those tears because it only shows your enemies are getting to you. And once they know they can get to you they will never stop."

Her words kicked my childhood survival instincts into gear, and I knew she was right. After our conversation, I understand it was Maxine who went into action and quietly utilized her underground sources to seek out the guilty culprit, who was eventually terminated from the sergeant's staff.

...

My husband Ron retired as a pharmacist after 16 years to take a management position with Computer Science Corporation (CSC), which oversees Medi-Cal health provider programs in California. Assemblyman Art Torres was the powerful chair of the Health Committee and was speaking at a health conference Ron attended. Art was looking for a principal health consultant to oversee Medi-Cal issues facing the state and wanted to talk to Ron about the position because of his health professional background and work experience with a Medi-Cal health provider.

At the same time, the number of family relatives working in the Assembly was rising and the Assembly Rules Committee, with the Speaker's approval, decided to send out a memo with specific hiring guidelines regarding nepotism.

Lo and behold, Art decided to hire Ron to fill the Medi-Cal position on his committee. When Ron excitedly told me of Art's offer, I responded, "You can't do that because we just sent out a memo limiting the hiring of relatives."

Ron dutifully reported back to Art that I told him he was unable to accept the position because it goes against the recent nepotism policy adopted by the Assembly. Art, who is not one to be denied, laughingly told Ron to speak with Papan and then Speaker Willie Brown to see if they would have a problem with his hiring. After both of them had a good laugh with Ron over the conversation, they indicated they had no problem with his hiring. Ron told Art there was no problem with Papan and the Speaker, it was just me who had the problem. Art told Ron, "Leave Maeley to me. I will take care of it."

Art knew I always had a hard time saying no to him because he was a mentor to me. Art strongly assured me that he would take the responsibility for the hiring of Ron so that it would not come back to bite me. Despite Art's assurance, I took a lot of criticism for the hiring. But I also made a lot of exceptions to the nepotism rules for many other legislators, so I just dealt with the criticism.

I have no regrets for the flak I took on behalf of Ron's appointment because that job opportunity proved to be invaluable to Ron's professional career.

Ron's expertise on health and Medi-Cal programs gained him great respect among the legislature. When Art Torres left the Assembly, the Speaker's chief of staff and health expert, Steve Thompson, recommended that Ron be appointed as the chief consultant to the Joint Legislative Committee on Medi-Cal. Subsequently, Ron left the Assembly to lobby for the California Hospital Association, and later served as one of the very few prominent Asian-American contract lobbyists in the Capitol for many years.

But for me, there were still other ceilings to break.

BREAKING THE GLASS CEILING

"Don't be afraid to fail, be afraid not to try."
—Michael Jordan

When Fred Taugher decided to leave the Chief Administrative Officer (CAO) position to join the private sector as a lobbyist, then Speaker Willie Brown had the authority to appoint the new CAO, with the approval of Rules Committee Chair Lou Papan. If it was solely Papan's choice, I believe he would have selected me to replace Fred because trust and loyalty were important to Papan. This highly sought position was the highest paid position in the Assembly during this time.

I did not get the CAO position. Instead, I ended up training three short-term CAO appointees selected by the Speaker: Tom Isaac, Richie Ross, and Rick Brandsma.

Every time a CAO departed, I was asked by colleagues and legislators when it was going to be my turn, as I continued to handle interim duties between vacancies. One would think that after seven years as a senior deputy I would be an heir apparent. But this is politics, and high-level appointments are not necessarily based on merit or seniority. I was a woman and an ethnic minority;

all the previous CAO's were white men. Would I be able to shatter this glass ceiling?

When Brandsma, the third CAO, decided to leave, he strongly encouraged me to go for the job. Bobbie Metzger, press secretary to the Speaker and my strongest ally in the Speaker's office, also suggested it was "my turn." When I discussed my dilemma with Papan, he indicated he had brought up the subject, but it would be up to me to convince the Speaker I could handle this position.

The morning of my meeting with the Speaker, I told my husband that when I returned home that evening I would either be the next CAO or I would be unemployed. As much as I loved my current job, my pride would not permit me to remain in the deputy's job to train yet another CAO.

Anyone who has ever worked for Speaker Willie Brown knows that when you meet with him, you have about 60 seconds to tell him the problem and another 60 seconds to provide him with solutions. Brown's philosophy is that he does not need people to advise him about problems; he wants people who can help him solve problems.

When we sat down, Brown asked the usual question, "What's the problem?" I told Brown I was interested in the CAO vacancy and if I had been good enough to train three CAO's during my seven years as the senior deputy, I should be good enough to have the job permanently.

Brown looked at me for what I considered the longest 30 seconds in my life, and simply said, "What took you so long?" Lesson learned.

With that, I became the first woman and the first ethnic minority ever to serve as the Chief Administrative Officer (CAO) of the California State Assembly, the highest paid position in the Assembly.

...

The recognition I received among the APIA communities in California for making political history in the state Capitol, at a time when my community was struggling and yearning to find a voice in state politics, was both gratifying and humbling. But now I had to prove myself worthy of the job.

My appointment was greeted with great support and accolades among my peers and legislators, because I would bring a continuity of management. The tutelage of former CAO's Taugher, Ross, and Brandsma was invaluable. Each brought their own strengths and management style to the job.

The Assembly CAO is the equivalent of the CEO of a private company, with a "board" of 80 elected members and responsibility for managing all the business functions and budget demands, as well as oversight of 1,200 staffers. The CAO oversees the committee bill referral process, which becomes extremely political because the ultimate success or failure of proposed legislation passing the legislature often depends on the policy committee hearing it.

The CAO is also responsible for ensuring that legislators manage their offices in a manner that would not invite undue public scrutiny nor be detrimental to the Assembly as an institution. I developed a keen intuition of knowing what behavior and practices would raise red flags and was the Rules chair's and Speaker's eyes and ears for potential problems. The late chief clerk Jim Driscoll and the late Legislative counsel Bion Gregory were invaluable advisors to me in this role.

When it came to administrative decisions involving both the Senate and the Assembly, I worked closely with the Senate chief executive officer, Cliff Berg, who was the most influential staff person in the Senate in those days. Cliff and I had a lot of freedom in handling mundane day-to-day details of Joint Rules Committee administrative issues involving both houses. (Cliff especially appreciated this arrangement because he preferred not having to deal with Papan's unpredictable temperament.) As a result, Cliff and I developed a mutually beneficial working relationship that eventually proved crucial to me during a time I was facing a serious career decision.

···

My toughest role as the CAO was trying to serve two drum majors who did not always march to the same beat.

Both Speaker Brown and Papan had extremely strong personalities, though with tremendous mutual affection and loyalty toward one another. When Brown took over as Speaker, many legislators wanted Papan replaced as Rules chairman. But the Speaker saw the value of having a strong person in the role, one who was feared by many.

Papan and Brown would play good cop/bad cop. In return, Papan repaid the Speaker tenfold by never hesitating to take whatever heat the Speaker threw at him.

There were times when each gave me a different approach or direction on a sensitive administrative problem, and I would have to find creative ways to appease both with a solution. When I was unable to resolve their differences, I simply told them to "duke it out" on their own.

I always felt that perhaps the greatest responsibility of legislative staff is to protect their bosses and help them succeed in their roles as legislators. The Speaker is elected every two years, which means he has to make sure he has enough member votes to be re-elected every two years. As the person in charge of handling administrative and personnel issues for all 80 members, I felt it was incumbent on me to protect the Speaker's leadership by being especially attentive to each legislator's needs.

As CAO, I felt it was my duty to make sure legislators were aware that the credit for special Assembly Rules favors being granted to them went to the Rules chair and the Speaker, whereas I would try to take responsibility for sensitive administrative decisions that went against legislators' requests

For example, every two years after the election, the CAO is responsible for assigning office space to legislators, pursuant to the Speaker's review and approval.

One year, the late Tom Hayden was very excited about his new office assignment because it had a backdoor entrance.

I was in a discussion with his then-wife, Oscar-winning actress and perennial activist Jane Fonda, who was selecting new carpets for the office, when I received a call from Papan that Gray Davis wanted this particular office. Davis had been especially helpful with the Speaker's campaign efforts that year. Papan wanted me to tell Hayden he must switch offices. I had to face Hayden and Fonda saying I had made a mistake by assigning to him an office which was to go to Davis. Hayden tried to get me to tell him the real reason, but I simply said that I erred. Luckily, Hayden and I had a solid relationship; I was very helpful to him during his tenure in the Capitol. He looked me in the eye and told me he was only giving up this office without a fight because I had to be the messenger bearing the news.

I felt even worse because Jane Fonda had given me two of her workout tapes that day.

...

Sometimes your best is still not enough.

My need to be liked forced me to face one of my greatest weaknesses: not standing up against those who, for whatever reason, wanted to damage my professional reputation.

Overall, I was popular with the legislators and most of the staff because I tried to treat everyone with the same care and attention no matter what position they held. However, I also experienced jealousy and resentment, which motivated some to want to see me fail.

As the adage goes: the higher you ascend the ladder, the more enemies you acquire.

...

When I was subjected to challenges by those who wanted me to fail, I chose to ignore the negative vibes and conduct business as usual.

Former Assemblyman and former San Francisco Mayor Art Agnos, as well as my former CAO Richie Ross, warned me that in politics it's all about strength. Until I demonstrated that there were consequences for those who wanted to harm me professionally and personally, I would never be fully respected as CAO. Both candidly told me my greatest weakness was needing to be liked, which I already realized.

This was put to the test when one of my own deputies tried to undermine me because he did not get the CAO position. We had become so close working together as deputies that I refused to believe staff warnings about the hostility he displayed towards me behind my back. But when I received a call from the majority leader telling me this deputy had overruled, without my knowledge, an order the Speaker personally had asked me to implement, I knew I had to act.

After I confided to Papan about the incident, he agreed that I had no choice but to terminate this individual. It was one of the most difficult actions I had to take. When it was over, my senior Assembly Rules staff was surprised; they said they didn't think I had the strength to fire a friend.

This reminded me anew of my first mentor's warning: it is better to be respected than to be liked.

When Papan decided to run for the state Senate in 1986, the Speaker named Assemblyman Tom Bane to be Papan's replacement as Assembly Rules chair. When Bane's appointment was announced, Bane immediately told me that he wanted me to stay on as the CAO. I considered Bane and his wife, Marlene, close friends, and I knew I would be able to work well with him. Then, a few weeks later, Bane told me in somber tones that the Speaker had someone else in mind for the CAO position. Bane urged me to talk to the Speaker personally if I wanted to remain in the position.

I was very aware I did not fit into Speaker Brown's inner circle of staffers who had been with him since his days as the chair of the Ways and Means committee. Steve Thompson, John Mockler, and Bob Connelly, among others, were much more comfortable being brash and outspoken around him. On occasions when I was in the Speaker's office with his staff, it was difficult for me to speak up because his aides were always fighting for "airtime," so I was hesitant to say anything. I let them talk over me. I was so in awe of the Speaker's brilliance, and so in need of his approval, that my lack of confidence became glaring, especially when he confronted me. Speaker Brown was the only person I worked for who intimidated me. He saw this as a weakness, and he was right. I had allowed myself to be defined by him.

I had no problem handling the challenging personalities of other legislators, and I certainly was capable of handling Papan's temper tantrums. But in front of Willie and his staff, I wilted.

I was devastated with the Speaker's decision to replace me considering how I had devoted myself to enhancing his leadership of the House. My damaged ego and wounded pride convinced me not to plead for my job. But I was determined for him to tell me face-to-face why he was replacing me. I met with Speaker Brown in his San Francisco office and he explained he would never be able to trust Bane the way he had trusted Papan. As insurance, he wanted to replace me with one of his old-time staff members, Bob Connelly, who he apparently felt would be more capable of handling Bane. He generously offered me another position in the Assembly as chief consultant of a new committee under the chairmanship of his most trusted ally in the house, Assemblyman Phil Isenberg, who was also the former mayor of Sacramento. I would even be able to keep my current CAO salary. The offer was tempting because of the deep respect I had for Isenberg, whom I considered among the most capable members in the Assembly. But I said no, thank you. After serving as the Chief Administrative

Officer of the Assembly, any other position in the Assembly would be seen as a demotion.

Since most of the legislators were unaware of my imminent departure, I confidentially turned to Isenberg for advice, because he sensed the rejection and loss of face I was feeling. For weeks, Isenberg patiently advised me to take my injured ego out of the equation and understand the move was not a referendum on my competence or accomplishments as the CAO; it was all about politics and I needed to move on.

With Isenberg's help, I took control of my next move. As legislators were hearing rumors of my leaving, many Democrats as well as Republican members wanted to talk to Brown about retaining me as CAO. But I did not want my departure to be an issue between them and the Speaker, so I assured my supporters that the decision to leave was mine, precipitated by Papan's departure.

Richie Ross, one of my former CAO bosses, graciously organized a grand farewell party for me attended by Assembly members, staff, and the third house of lobbyists. Willie Brown and I had our official moment of farewell. I told him publicly that working for him was one of the greatest experiences I could ever ask for because, if I could work for him, I could work for anyone, and I meant every word.

...

The Assembly had been my home for 13 years, and I was still hurting both about leaving my position and my personal secretary, Grace Yee, whom I loved, and my excellent executive staff, Sharon Usher, Sam Walton, and Gus Demas, to name a few. But, once again, I forced myself to look at the positive side of this experience and change. I was so fortunate I had the opportunity to work for two of California's greatest Assembly Speakers, Leo McCarthy and Willie Brown. I grew and learned from a mentor whose trust, loyalty, and support allowed me to become the first woman and ethnic minority to serve as the Chief Administrative Officer of the

Assembly, Lou Papan, the same Lou Papan who had asked me in my interview, "Why aren't you working at the cosmetic counter for your husband's drugstore?"

In hindsight, the Speaker's decision was a blessing in disguise. At this juncture I was at the height of my political activism, touted by *Asian Week* as the most "influential non-elected Asian Pacific political leader in California."

The Asian American political scene was going to change my future.

Assembly farewell party with Speaker Willie Brown; Assembly Rules Committee. From left to right: Assemblymembers Lucy Killea, Phil Isenberg, Tom Bane, Chief Clerk Jim Driscoll (behind Maeley), Lou Papan (behind him sgt. at arms), Secretary Grace Yee, Assemblymembers Stan Statham, Bill Filante and Sunny Mojonnier

MOVING UP

"When one door closes, another door opens."
—Alexander Graham Bell

As it turned out, the timing of my departure from the Assembly could not have been better.

My Senate counterpart, Cliff Berg, saw an opportunity to recruit me to work for the Senate. He convinced Senate President Pro Tem David Roberti that, with no Asian state legislators in the Capitol, the fast-growing APIA constituency lacked a presence in the Legislature and this was a good time for the Senate to serve this constituency by creating a Senate Office of Asian-Pacific Affairs. Berg was familiar with the statewide efforts Georgette Imura and I were working on with the APIA communities. From time to time, he would ask for our assistance when one of the Senate members needed help with his or her APIA constituencies. Since Georgette and I were already known political entities, Berg felt that hiring the both of us would give the office instant statewide credibility.

After spending 13 years with the Assembly (1974-87), I was eagerly looking forward to continuing my political career in the Senate, pursuing my passion of working with my community in an official capacity with my best friend, Georgette.

Georgette and I looked at each other with great excitement. "Can you believe we're going to get paid for doing something we've been doing for free for the past decade?" she said.

The services we had provided as legislative staff were now formally sanctioned by the creation of this Senate office of Asian Pacific Affairs during a time when there was no APIA representation in the state Legislature. The office was to fill the gap by serving as a liaison between California's APIA constituency and the Senate. The office would also serve as an information resource to senators who called for advice and counsel regarding APIA issues affecting their districts.

As a result of the APIA networks we had created with the Asian Legislative staff caucus, our office became the instant gathering place for all APIA local elected officials and community leaders visiting the Capitol, as well as a gathering hub for the APIA legislative staffers and APIA candidates looking for jobs in the Capitol.

It was during this period that I first met Maria Hsia, a young Taiwanese businesswoman and immigration specialist based in Los Angeles. Maria was an active fundraiser for March Fong Eu and Lt. Governor Leo McCarthy when he was running for the U.S Senate. We met during an Asian community event and she often sought my advice on which legislators were supportive of our community issues. Whenever she was in Sacramento, she would drop by and invite me to many of her social or fundraising events. She introduced me to John Huang, a banker, who came from Taiwan in his youth and graduated from the University of Connecticut with an MBA specializing in banking. John was an executive with the Lippo Bank, owned by the Riady family in Indonesia. When I met him, he was also the president of the Chinese American Bankers Association in Los Angeles. John would invite Georgette and me to Los Angeles community events, and also seek our advice about legislative issues affecting the APIA community. Both were avid supporters of Sen. Roberti for establishing the Office of Asian Pacific Affairs.

Maria, with the help of John Huang, formed the Pacific Leadership PAC fund composed of Asian American business executives, some of whom had businesses both in the U.S. and China. Eventually, Maria and John escalated their political involvement to the national level through the Democratic National Committee, Democratic Senate Campaign Committee, and presidential campaigns. By this time, I had developed a personal friendship with both Maria and John—which later became newsworthy, due to unfortunate circumstances.

More about this in a later chapter. It's what I previewed in the opening pages of this book.

...

Our office undertook some major issues that resonated with the APIA community during this period under the authority of the Senate, except for the Lungren issue, which we undertook on our own as volunteers. These included:

U.C. Admission policies against APIA students: We alerted Senator Roberti to the sudden changes in the U.C. admissions requirements in the late 80s, which appeared biased against Asian applicants because of their increasing enrollment numbers on the U.C. campuses. Senator Roberti requested that the auditor general examine the sudden changes in the admission requirements, and the results forced the U.C. President to modify the changes because of the lack of adequate notification.

Japanese Redress and Sanrio's Black Sambo racial uproar: Georgette took the lead in helping with a number of Japanese redress-related bills by generating community support for the legislation. This office played a major role assisting the Japanese American Citizens League (JACL) national director Ron Wakabayashi, to squelch a racism charge and a boycott by the African American community over Japan's Sanrio toy company when they added Black

Sambo figures to their Hello Kitty collection. The Black Sambo figures were immediately discontinued, and a cultural educational exchange program was established between Japan and the U.S. which is still ongoing today.

The Vietnamese Fishermen's battle to eliminate a 200-year-old federal ban on non-citizens owning or piloting commercial fishing vessels in California waters:

Commercial fishing was one of the primary means of income for the large number of unskilled Vietnamese immigrants arriving in California. However, they were prohibited from owning pilot commercial fishing vessels because many of them were still waiting to become citizens. We spent months teaching this community how to use the political process to overturn this archaic federal ban. Thanks to Congressman Norman Mineta, the ban was eventually overturned by Congress in 1990. This marked the Vietnamese community's first successful encounter in politics and since that time they have never looked back. This experience inspired many young Vietnamese leaders to get involved politically and the current number of Vietnamese Americans holding elected office is growing at a more rapid pace than any other Asian ethnic group today.

Assisting foreign-trained health professionals seeking licensure in California, and Filipino War Veterans: Our office developed a very close working relationship with the Filipino American communities. Sen. Roberti was a strong champion of providing a pathway for foreign trained health professionals from the Philippines seeking state licensure to practice in California. Georgette and I worked closely with the Filipino grand dames of Democratic politics, Alice Bulos and Cynthia Bonta, and others to fight for the veteran benefits for the Filipino War Veterans who helped the U.S. troops during World War II.

1990 Kennedy/Simpson Immigration Reform Act: The 1965 Immigration Reform Act enabled an unprecedented number of

Asians to immigrate to this country to make up for the decades of discriminatory immigration policies against Asians in the past. Included in this act was the ability for the new Asian immigrant citizens to sponsor immediate family members to join them in the U.S. The Kennedy/Simpson immigration reform act going through Congress in 1990 included language regarding the discontinuation of family reunification benefits in the bill, which meant that newly immigrant citizens would no longer be able to sponsor their parents or siblings to join them in the U.S. Today they call it chain migration.

A national group of APIA immigrations experts, Bill Hing and Ignatius Bau of California and Stanley Mark of New York, worked with a coalition of APIA, Hispanic, and Jewish immigration coalitions to develop a strategy to modify this bill to protect its family reunification language.

But it was an uphill battle to go against a bi-partisan bill being carried by Sen. Ted Kennedy and Republican Sen. Alan Simpson. And unlike other ethnic minority and special interest groups, the APIA lacked any national organization that had the access and influence in Congress to lobby this bill.

Sen. Roberti generously allowed me to join a coalition of APIA civil rights leaders who traveled to Washington D.C. to lobby for the extension of family reunification clause. Immigration attorney Gordon Quan from Houston (who later became the Mayor of Houston); Yvonne Lee, prominent Chinese civil rights leader representing the Chinese American Citizens Alliance; Rev. Norman Fong, who represented the Chinese religious communities of San Francisco Chinatown; and Melinda Yee, National Director of the Organization of Chinese Americans, the largest Chinese American organization in the U.S. were members of this coalition.

Our coalition was unable to gain access to meet with key senators until we joined efforts with my friends John Huang and Maria Hsia members of the Pacific Leadership PAC Fund which contributed heavily to the Democratic Senate Campaign

Committee. Their relationships with Democratic U.S. senators enabled our group to get face-to-face meetings with eight key senators serving on the Judiciary Committee.

Even more remarkable: we were able to meet with Sen. Ted Kennedy for two hours who was open to listening to our position.

At the same time, the APIA and Latino immigration rights communities conducted a massive ethnic media and grassroots write-in campaign hitting the districts of key congressional votes in both houses. The result of this united effort produced compromise language on the family reunification amendment.

This remarkable victory had Congressman Alan Simpson begrudgingly acknowledging on the Senate floor that Asians had finally learned how to make their voices heard in Congress: "Never before has the Asian community been so galvanized… They know how it works…fundraisers, office calls, the whole works, and I'm going to give them a grade A."

Unfortunately, those of us who represented the civil rights and grassroots communities had a reality check on how Congress works: money buys access.

When Congressman Daniel Lungren was nominated for state treasurer by Governor George Deukmejian, Congressman Robert Matsui approached Georgette and me to discuss why Asian Americans should oppose Lungren's nomination. Lungren served on the Commission on Wartime Relocation and Internment of Civilians in 1980, and Matsui never forgave Lungren for introducing bogus claims about Japanese American spies during the hearings, an action Matsui felt was a deliberate attempt to subvert the Commission's work.

Matsui stressed that for our APIA communities to be taken seriously, we must demonstrate that there are consequences to be paid when our community is shamelessly disrespected publicly. Georgette and I considered this our marching orders and discussed this with our boss Senator Roberti, who was a strong civil rights advocate. His response was, what we do on our own time is up to us, but it cannot be part of the office activity since Lungren's confirmation has be approved by the Senate.

Georgette and I turned to a small cadre of California's best-known APIA civil rights attorneys led by Don Tamaki, Dale Minami, Hoyt Zia, John Ota, and Chinese for Affirmative Action Executive Director Henry Der, to lead the battle. Lungren's ultra-conservative voting record showed that he supported many issues that negatively affected a broad base of California's constituencies, including women, seniors, labor, environmentalists, gays, and ethnic minorities.

During the evenings and weekends, Georgette and I advised this opposition group on how to galvanize these constituency groups into communicating their opposition to Lungren's appointment to their senate representatives. Bill Wong, a recent U.C. Davis grad who was interested in getting involved with politics, volunteered to help with the effort. He devoted endless hours to serve as the communication link among all the opposition forces within and outside the state Capitol.

Lungren lost the nomination by one vote (Senator Quentin Kopp's) on the Senate floor.

The *Washington Post* declared, "The sudden emergence of Asian American influence in the Lungren controversy is the most obvious of several signs of the growing political clout for a minority with only 7 percent of the state's population. In the last few months, they have revolutionized the political image of what once was California's quietest minority." Congressman Bob Matsui proudly proclaimed, "This was the first time the APIA community stood up and made an impact on a statewide political decision."

The Lungren campaign was Bill Wong's first major venture in politics, and after this effort Bill was hooked on politics forever. He demonstrated such a passion for it that we encouraged him to apply for a Senate fellowship. After he successfully completed the program and started his legislative career, Georgette and I knew he would be among the first to break barriers to become a successful and respected Asian American political consultant of this era. Today Bill serves as the political director to California Assembly Speaker Anthony Rendon.

Later, Lungren won election as California's attorney general—and, to his credit, he hired a number of Asian Americans to serve in key positions on his staff.

...

Roberti's office of Asian Pacific Affairs was bi-partisan. We assisted the late Matt Fong with his senate confirmation to serve on the State Board of Equalization, his entrance into state politics, where he subsequently became state treasurer. Lester Lee also sought our counsel regarding his attempt to be appointed to the U.C. Board of Regents but, unfortunately, he was not confirmed. We also assisted Leslie Tang Schilling as she went through her successful appointment process to the U.C. Board of Regents.

However, in 1990, with the passage of Proposition 140 mandating a 40 per cent cut in the state legislative budget and imposing term limits on legislators, our advocacy office was among the first to be cut. It was deemed expendable as new Asian legislators in the Assembly were positioned to become the institutional voice of the APIA in the state Capitol.

The APIA community's enthusiastic response to the Senate Office of Asian Pacific Affairs and its growing awareness of the value of political engagement helped to awaken a sleeping dragon that was no longer content to be invisible.

We saw the emergence of a silent minority group growing stronger and more visible during this era. We saw the emboldened civil rights and protest movements evolve in defense against criminal injustices involving the imprisonment of Chol So Lee, the spy allegation against Wen Ho Lee, and the tragic murder in

Detroit of Vincent Chin. We saw more APIA faces in the Capitol and more APIA candidates running for public office.

As for me, this experience of working with my best friend to help politically empower our own community was the most rewarding professional and personal experience of my lifetime. Georgette's friendship changed my life from the moment I met her. Many of our accomplishments throughout the years would not have been possible without her strength, vision, and determination. While I was the person who tried to please everyone, she was the one who was direct and kept her eye on the ball. She never cared about recognition or who was the lead, she simply wanted to get the job done. Between us, Georgette's character and personal background made her the stronger and more confident one. We complemented one another and nothing was ever too challenging for us as long as we worked together.

Senate Pres. pro tem David Roberti, Georgette Imura, and attorney Jerry Chong, during my tenure as COS to Roberti

A SURPRISE OPPORTUNITY

Senate President Pro Tem David Roberti's chief of staff duties were managed by Nancy Burt, one of Roberti's closest advisors and a senior political operative. As a result of the passage of Proposition 140 in 1990, which mandated budget cuts and term limits for State legislators, the fear of staff layoffs loomed over the state Capitol.

Nancy was leaning toward retirement, and generously used this opportunity to leave so that a job could be saved by promoting someone from the staff to take her place. Nancy's legendary reputation and skill as a tough, politically savvy campaign veteran earned her a solid reputation with many senior senators, and it was difficult to predict who among Roberti's talented senior staff would succeed her.

Most of Roberti's leadership team joined him when he became Senate President pro tem and there was very little turnover. Each member of his leadership staff was recruited into highly defined roles that showcased individual expertise. In fact, the combined experience and skills of Roberti's team created one of the most efficient and tightly organized President pro tem staffs in the Senate's history, which contributed to Roberti's long leadership tenure.

When Nancy Burt called me in to let me know that I was selected to take her place, I was speechless and asked, "Why me?" when there were far more seasoned Roberti staffers who had more seniority and tenure with Roberti. Her explanation was that Roberti needed someone who had the ability to effectively communicate with 40 senate members from both sides of the aisle, in addition to managing the leadership staff. She said my reputation as the Assembly CAO convinced them that, if I was able to manage the more chaotic membership of the lower house and work effectively with leadership of both the Republicans and Democrats as well as manage the house, I could do the same job for Roberti in the Senate.

This time, however, I would be serving a boss I barely knew.

The second challenge before me was how I was going to establish myself as the manager of Roberti's leadership staff with people who had far more experience working with Roberti on a personal, policy, and political level?

Georgette was appointed to the Senate Elections and Reapportionment Committee staff to help with the reapportionment challenge facing the legislature. She subsequently was promoted by Roberti to become his Senate floor manager, overseeing legislative activity on his behalf during Senate floor sessions.

. . .

Senator Roberti was a completely different personality from my former bosses, Speaker Willie Brown and Rules Chair Lou Papan.

Roberti was a very private person who was somewhat shy, soft spoken, and much harder to read than Brown or Papan. The common denominators between Brown and Roberti as leaders of their respective houses was that they were both brilliant, skilled orators and savvy political strategists. However, their management styles were as different as night and day.

The Speaker of the Assembly focused more on managing the political dynamics of the house versus overseeing policy issues and was far more socially engaged with his members. Senate President pro tem Roberti was third in line for succession to the Governor's seat, and the Senate was responsible for the confirmation of Governor's appointees, which gave the Senate leader more power than the Speaker of the Assembly. But Speaker Brown was the celebrity.

The senators differed from the Assembly members because they were considered more seasoned and traditional, with professional decorum and shared relationships. Most of the senators during this era had first served in the Assembly. Therefore, Senator Roberti faced less drama among the personalities of his House and his leadership style was more consensus oriented. As a result, there was less partisan bickering in the Senate. This allowed Senator Roberti to focus more on policy issues, his primary passion.

As his new staff director, I realized I had a steep learning curve to understand Roberti's personality, priorities, relationships, and policy goals. I quickly realized that his lengthy tenure as president pro tem derived from his Teddy Roosevelt style of leading ("Speak softly and carry a big stick"). I learned that Roberti did not hesitate to use his power to demonstrate his leadership strength in the Senate when needed, but rarely had to do so because of his reputation for fairness. Fairness thus was highly respected by senators on both sides of the aisle.

The first thing I did was to hire an executive assistant who had the experience and skills to help me navigate "Robertiland," and I was fortunate to have Bobbie Sardo perform that role. My next step was to reach out to Roberti's most trusted lieutenants, starting with those who helped get him elected, such as Jerry Zanelli, Cliff Berg, and Nancy Burt. Mel Assagai and Lori Snell were his closest personal staff. I wanted to learn all I could about his instincts, priorities, political relationships, and personality traits.

In terms of Roberti's politics, I relied on Steve Coony and Cathy Keig to counsel me on campaign priorities. I turned to the late Bob

Forsythe and to Steve Glazer to understand Roberti's preferences on media exposure and press relationships. And for policy priorities, I reached out to Roberti's veteran staff, including Simon Haines, Donna Brownsey, Nettie Sabelhaus, and David Panush to educate me on issues and the budget so I had an overall grasp of his positions. I also relied on the friendships I enjoyed with Roberti's advocacy team which included Roy Perez, to keep me apprised of special interest constituencies Roberti most cared about.

Bottom line: through my outreach to the Roberti executive staff, I conveyed the vision for my new role. I saw myself serving as a liaison between the Senate members and Roberti as well as facilitating communication between Roberti and his leadership team. Roberti was a thinker, not a talker, and did not enjoy a lot of meetings, so I was able to fill this void. To this day, I feel so grateful and privileged to have worked with Roberti's team, who never hesitated to counsel or advise me on issues, as well as accept my guidance whenever necessary to ensure that Roberti's goals and priorities as Senate leader were met.

It was easier for me to work with the Senate members because there were only 40 of them versus 80 in the Assembly. The senators also tended to manage their offices independently, like little fiefdoms, and were less demanding of leadership. In the beginning, I experienced some reluctance from a few of the older white male senators and senior policy consultants who were noticeably uncomfortable dealing with an Asian female in this position of influence. A couple of these members were condescending when they talked to me, and one 80-year-old senator barely made eye contact when I met with him. But I was able to overcome this type of behavior in the Assembly and no longer allowed this type of behavior to affect my dignity or self-respect.

...

After 20 years in the building, and with Roberti forced out by new term limits, I decided it was time for me to experience life outside the Capitol. My departure was made easier when I picked a great replacement for my position, Kathy Bowler, who was a dynamic state Democratic Party executive and well known to the Roberti staff.

Being able to conclude my Capitol career by serving David Roberti as his chief of staff was a badge of honor. His courage as the first state legislator to author a bill to ban assault weapons, which subjected him to a recall campaign and death threats, was historic and demonstrated his foresight in seeing how citizens' access to assault weapons could wreak havoc on our society.

Unfortunately, his vision became a reality.

My 20 years of Capitol experience was like a boot camp of life's traumas, excitement, challenges, disappointments, accomplishments, fame, notoriety, great fun, and struggles, rolled up into one adventure. What job allows one to learn from some of the most highly respected intellectual, academic, policy, and political minds in the State Legislature? Being able to interact with high profile elected officials at the state and federal level provided me with the ultimate gift of access, influence, and relationships that I continue to share with all of those who strive for the same dream today.

FROM WASHINGTON TO RETIREMENT

"I was once afraid of people saying, 'Who does she think she is?' Now I have the courage to stand and say, 'This is who I am.'"
—Oprah Winfrey

At the time of my retirement from the state Capitol, I was at the height of my political engagement with national APIA politics. I was advocating for more APIA involvement with politics at all levels.

During my involvement with the first Bill Clinton presidential campaign, I was introduced by John Huang to his boss, James Riady. The Riady family owned the Lippo Group, which was among the most diversified conglomerates in Asia, based in Indonesia. The Riady family had business ties in Arkansas during the time Clinton was governor, which resulted in a close personal friendship between James Riady and the Clintons.

James Riady was a true philanthropist with strong Christian values who believed in contributing to humanitarian and social causes in Asia and abroad. He seemed genuinely perplexed as to why Asian Americans were not more highly involved in American politics. He generously supported organizational efforts to strengthen the political voice of Asian Americans in the U.S.

He saw the work I did to help educate and galvanize the Asian American vote for the Clinton campaign and he saw how this community's support for Clinton was rewarded by the significant number of high level Asian American appointments into the Clinton administration.

When I was deciding career options as I was preparing to retire from the State, John Huang asked if I would consider a part-time contract paid by one of the Lippo subsidiaries to continue my work advocating and educating the APIA communities about the importance of political and civic engagement. I agreed to do so if it didn't conflict with my future career move.

I had received a number of lobbying offers during my years at the Capitol. However, having served as the CAO of the Assembly and chief of staff to the Senate President pro tem, I was accustomed to being an insider capable of providing access to power rather than seeking access from outside the Capitol dome.

The most interesting offer came from late Democratic National Committee Chair Ron Brown on the eve of President Clinton's first election victory. An emotional and excited Brown called to thank me for my help with the campaign and then asked me to consider coming to Washington D.C. in some capacity to help Clinton make good on his promise of including Asian Americans as a part of his White House staff and administration.

With my daughter in college, I asked my husband Ron how he would feel about a commuter marriage since he had no intention of giving up his lucrative lobbying position in California. In his usual direct and decisive manner, Ron informed me that if I accepted a full-time position in Washington, he and his "new wife" would wish me the best of luck.

For a brief moment, I was excited to think I might be able to continue my career at the highest professional and political level in Washington D.C. But the reality was that sacrificing my marriage and family was not an option; family priorities had been sacrificed enough during my years at the state Capitol.

At the same time, I met a prominent Washington D.C. lobbyist, Mark Cowan, who was visiting the Capitol to accept a Senate resolution on behalf of a client. Mark was impressed to see an Asian American woman serving as the chief of staff to the California Senate president pro tem and was also impressed with the number of members I knew in the California congressional delegation. After our meeting, he called me to see if I would be interested in establishing a California office for Cassidy & Associates, which was rated as the number one privately owned lobbying firm in Washington at the time. The California office would help service California-based clients, as well as help market new clients here.

After a successful meeting with Gerry Cassidy, the founder, and Jim Fabiani, the President of the firm, I understood there would still be occasional travel required between Sacramento and Washington, but at my discretion. I was still hesitant about the commute. But Mark Cowan was able to sweeten the offer with a generous six-figure salary, a senior vice president title, and an agreement that I would still be allowed to service the Lippo contract.

Moving from the state Capitol arena to work for Cassidy & Associates was a total culture change for this California girl, who was so comfortable in her established role in Sacramento. Cassidy & Associates employed over 100 high-profile professional lobbyists and a public relations team headquartered in a luxurious office building at 700 13th Street, in the heart of Washington's lobbying scene. This was definitely a different type of pressure, work style, and pace compared to Sacramento.

Meeting the executives and senior professionals of the firm was even more overwhelming as many were former members of Congress, former congressional chiefs of staff, retired generals, and former cabinet members of various administrations. The public relations arm of C&A was headed by political giants Jody Powell and Sheila Tate, formerly with the Carter and Reagan administrations, respectively, and included famed Democratic campaign consultant Bob Beckel.

There definitely was a lack of diversity at the firm. There was one other female vice president and three senior women managers, one African American senior VP/chief counsel, Greg Gill, and one big personality, Hawaiian Henry Guigni, who previously served as U.S. Senator Dan Inouye's chief of staff before he became chief Sergeant at Arms of the U.S. Senate. Giugni left the Senate to become vice chair of Cassidy and Associates and was one of the biggest rainmakers for the firm, thanks to his close relationships with U.S. senators, including Inouye. And because of Guigni's and Inouye's ties to Hawaii, Cassidy and Associates represented a large number of Hawaii's largest industry clients as well as the state of Hawaii itself.

Fortunately for me, Henry Guigni was so excited to see an Asian American professional woman join the firm that he instantly took me under his wing. His friendship and support were a gift; his guidance was invaluable as I faced a very competitive work environment where you are only as good as the last client you brought in the door.

During my first month, and to the amazement of the staff, the chairman of Cassidy & Associates, Gerry Cassidy, asked me to accompany him to the Capitol for a meeting. Cassidy shrewdly wanted me to be with him because he knew how close I was with former Assemblyman and now House Majority Caucus Leader Vic Fazio.

From that moment on, I got it. My value would be my relationships with members of Congress' largest delegation, from California. The majority of the California House members at that time came from the Legislature.

...

There were very few Asian Americans lobbying in Washington and I definitely was an anomaly.

When I arranged meetings on the Hill with the California delegation members, I was generally able to get one-on-one meetings with the congress member because of our relationship in Sacramento. This was impressive to my colleagues at Cassidy because lobbyists are routinely delegated to meet only with staff.

However, I was amused that when I would arrive with my team, associates from the firm, the reception staff would automatically assume I was staff and would ask my white male counterparts if they were "Tom," as in "Tom Maeley."

At politically charged social events, it was different—a very clubby, mainly white, whom-you-know environment, where everyone was looking to talk to the most politically connected person in the room. There definitely was a lack of Asian presence at such events. I felt awkward trying to make small talk with strangers who were obviously puzzled that an unknown Asian American woman carried the title of Senior Vice President of Cassidy & Associates. I was used to having a political identity in California, but in Washington I had none. I found myself fighting for acceptance not only among the influential clients and Washington power brokers, but also among colleagues at Cassidy who'd never worked with an Asian American female before and were curious to see if I would succeed or fail.

...

When I arrived in 1994, Cassidy's biggest client was from the Taiwan Republic of China. The organization was lobbying Congress to grant a temporary visa allowing Taiwan President Lee Teng Hui to set foot on U.S. soil to accept an honorary award from his alma mater, Cornell University. Because the U.S. had no diplomatic relations with Taiwan, based on the One China policy, Taiwan's president was not allowed to visit the U.S. in any official capacity.

My first assignment was to rally Taiwanese American supporters in the U.S. to write their representatives supporting a resolution allowing the Taiwan president's visit. I was able to use my national APIA network to generate ethnic press coverage and connect with key Taiwan supporters from various states to lobby their congress members on this issue.

Gerry Warburg, a former staffer with Sen. Alan Cranston, was the lead on this campaign, and our team delivered a huge victory for Cassidy & Associates when Congress adopted our resolution to allow President Lee Teng Hui a one-time visit to the United States.

Mark Cowan and Jim Fabiani, president of the firm, were known for their keen marketing skills and abilities in bringing in million-dollar clients. Being a part of the California marketing team, which included Bill Press, former California Democratic Party chair and media commentator, was a learning experience for me. I discovered how to research and target needs of potential clients and then to connect those needs to the firm's expertise and services.

Eventually, I was able to help bring in clients such as Panda Express, Charter Properties, California Science Center, City of San Francisco, Cargico Engineering, Cray Research, City of South Pasadena, San Francisco Independent Publishers, as well as some international clients from Asia in need of crisis management services provided by our public relations team of Powell and Tate.

Ultimately, my greatest value to Cassidy was my relationships with the California congressional delegation. After five years of learning how to navigate the D.C. scene, the rigorous work schedules and lifestyle, the constant pressure to bring in clients, and the demanding East Coast/West Coast commute began to wear on me.

Cassidy & Associates was also undergoing some turbulence of its own. Mark Cowan and other friends had left.

My dear friend, David Kim, who handled diversity marketing strategy for Anheuser Busch, encouraged me to start my own firm and was willing to offer me my first independent contract helping Anheuser Busch with its diversity outreach program. I negotiated a generous transition package with Cassidy where I would continue to service clients I brought into the firm as an independent contractor and then add Anheuser Busch as the first corporate client of Tom & Associates.

...

The transition to owning my own company forced me to learn how to market the firm by placing appropriate value on my experience, influence, and relationships to decision makers when pricing a contract. It meant throwing that Asian humility out the window and having confidence in what I would be able to deliver to the client.

Tom and Associates flourished with a combined revenue of Ron's contract as a senior lobbyist with Governmental Advocates, Inc., and my list of clients, which included Fortune 500 companies, non- profit and political organizations, and clients from Asia.

In 2002, when my one and only grandchild, Maxwell Martinez, was born, I decided to retire to spend time helping raise my grandson, which also allowed me to compensate for the many years I was not available to raise my daughter full-time. It was one of the best decisions I ever made. Thanks to Ron's shrewd fiscal planning, we have been able to enjoy financial security, enabling us to retire early enough to appreciate life at its fullest with more time for family and to give back.

However, my passion to help APIA elected officials, candidates, and young APIA professionals has never waned. My involvement in expanding the voice of Asian Americans in all aspects of the American way of life continues.

My five years at Cassidy had expanded my professional horizons to a level that I never imagined, both financially, politically, and professionally. Lobbying in Washington was another arena in which Asian Americans were seen as anomalies and I had the burden to prove my relevancy and value in my role as a Washington lobbyist. I thank Mark Cowan for his belief in my being able to add value to Cassidy & Associates; I thank my beloved big brother, the late Henry Giugni, for his encouragement on how to survive the pressures and demands of the firm; and to Victoria Lion Monroe and Peggy Bowen, thank you for being the only two women in the firm to befriend me as the only professional minority woman in this firm.

I also will be forever indebted to Chairman of the Board Gerry Cassidy who stood by me during one of the most tumultuous times of my life. His loyalty and counsel, and the support his staff provided during the 1997 campaign finance scandal, was partially responsible for helping me survive that painful experience—the subject of a later chapter.

BOOK THREE

Waking the Sleeping Dragon

*"Every moment is an organizing opportunity, every person a
potential activist, every minute a chance to change the world."*
—Dolores Huerta

UNDER THE CAPITOL DOME

During the 70s, Asian Americans, primarily Chinese, Japanese, and Korean, were lumped into one category. All Asian Americans were considered academically accomplished, economically advantaged, model citizens...and politically impotent.

There were many reasons why political recognition eluded this community: historical discrimination practices barring the Asians from voting and the naturalization process which eluded them until recent generations, chief among them.

These Asian sub-ethnic groups separated by cultural histories and historical rivalries factionalized these communities against one another, resulting in each sub-ethnic Asian group seeking its own identity versus uniting under one major ethnic identification.

Asian families immigrating to this country were more preoccupied with economic survival, education, financial security, and the value of self-perseverance, which left little time for politics. More important, most of the new immigrants fled to this country to escape tyrannical governments, which made them that much more reluctant to engage in government, politics, and the public sphere.

Even early Asian American elected trailblazers, such as California Senator Al Song and Assemblywoman and former California Secretary of State March Fong Eu, who were both

Democrats, found it difficult to empower their own community, because the Asian voter base was incapable of delivering a large block of votes. Voter participation was low, compounded by the fact that the small percentage of Asian American voters leaned slightly Republican between the two major parties.

During this period, Georgette and I were aware of our good fortune to be among the small number of Asian Americans working in the state Legislature.

Georgette worked for an African American legislator and I worked for a Latino legislator. We saw how they each fought for issues and resources affecting their respective communities. As Asian Americans, we became increasingly aware and dismayed that our own ethnic community was invisible and voiceless within the halls of the Capitol.

We also realized that the Asian American community identification was limited to the majority Chinese, Japanese, and Korean populations, leaving out Filipino Americans, Pacific Islanders, South Asians, and Indian Americans. Therefore, Georgette and I started to use the term Asian Pacific Islander Americans (APIA) to be more inclusive in the identity of our entire community (this is the term I will be using throughout the book when I am discussing the general APIA population).

To help elevate the APIA presence in the state Capitol, we decided to form the Asian Pacific Legislative Staff Caucus (APLSC), composed of a small cadre of professional APIA staffers in the building, including Larry Asera, Sarah Reyes Kim, Colin Chiu, Debra Nakatomi, Florence Ochi, Terrence Terauchi, Joyce Iseri, and Dale Shimasaki. We also reached out to APIA staffers who worked in legislative district offices, such as Mike Woo, before he became a L.A. City councilman, Audrey Noda who worked for Assemblyman Art Torres, and Lynn Choy Uyeda, who was a field director for Speaker Leo McCarthy.

Together, we developed a workshop that demystified the legislative process and used it to educate local APIA community organizations on the importance of political engagement and how to effectively advocate in Sacramento. We also tried to recruit more APIA candidates to seek jobs or paid fellowships in the Capitol by sharing our work experiences and the rewards of serving in the State Legislature.

...

At that time, there were very few APIA community leaders who understood the importance of political engagement. But Georgette and I found that Ron Wakabayashi, national director of the Japanese American Citizens League, and Henry Der, executive director of Chinese for Affirmative Action based in San Francisco, and Warren Furutani, a highly respected community leader in Los Angeles, were among the most trusted and respected Asian community leaders in California. We asked them to help us connect with community organizations as well as advise us on key issues impacting the APIA communities.

As we met with community groups representing the various geographic regions and sub-ethnic groups, there was an obvious hunger to learn about the legislative and political process, to the point that Georgette and I could barely keep up with the demands for the workshop. The response and feedback refuted the general attitude held by state legislators that APIA voters were indifferent to politics.

Georgette and I decided that the information we were collecting from these community workshops would be helpful to legislators representing these districts. Much to our pleasant surprise, this feedback was welcomed in the Capitol, where legislators confessed to being unaware of APIA issues.

As the Asian Pacific Legislative Staff Caucus (APLSC) grew, it also became a mentor network for many APIA community members who were interested in getting politically involved. More young APIA were recruited into working for the State Legislature either at the State Capitol or in district offices, and more APIA college graduates enlisted in the prestigious Senate and Assembly fellowship programs as an entry pathway to future careers in the state Legislature.

Georgette and I, with the members of the APLSC, felt strongly that we needed a mechanism to groom high school youth to learn and understand the value of public service and political engagement, as well as help provide them with self-esteem and leadership skills. APLSC created the Asian Pacific Youth Leadership program, a three-day experience in the state Capitol, for statewide high school candidates to experience their first exposure to state government in action. The program continues to flourish and is managed by the current generation of legislative staff members and former legislative staff members of the Legislature.

As of today, approximately 1,800 students have attended this program. Many graduates have moved on to professional positions in public service, including a number of whom were subsequently elected to local offices. Eventually, as more Asian legislators were elected in the mid-1980s onward, the Legislature formally established the Asian Pacific Legislative Caucus, comprising elected APIA legislators and salaried consultant staff. This caucus took over the role of the Asian Pacific Legislative Staff Caucus that Georgette and I started.

Today, the Asian Pacific Legislative Staff Caucus has been renamed the Asian Pacific Islander Capitol Association (APICA) and focuses on staff career development and recruitment and works with other ethnic staff caucuses to raise the awareness of diversity issues in the state Capitol.

Before Assemblywoman Judy Chu left her APIA legislative caucus chair position in the Legislature to serve in Congress, she saw a need to create a non-profit arm of the APIA Legislative Caucus called the

Joint Asian Pacific Islander Legislative Caucus Institute. The Institute would provide educational summits and sponsor cultural events on behalf of the state's APIA constituency in the state Capitol. I was asked to serve as its founding president, with Georgette as vice president and treasurer, and Dale Shimasaki as secretary.

The Institute created the Capitol Academy, whose mission was to identify the best and brightest local APIA elected officials and provide them a three-day boot camp experience in the state Capitol, teaching them how to become effective legislators. A number of the Academy graduates went on to win seats in the Assembly and Senate. Today, many of the current APIA Legislative Caucus members are graduates of the Capitol Academy, which has expanded its training programs to train mid-level, seasoned legislative staffers to ascend into senior and executive positions within the Capitol and state government under the leadership of Annie Lam, the executive director of the Institute and a former legislative staff member to former Assemblyman Mike Eng.

During the time Georgette and I were organizing the Asian Pacific Legislative Staff Caucus activities, Assemblyman Paul Bannai a Republican, and newly elected Democrat Assemblyman Floyd Mori both became actively engaged in supporting and guiding our empowerment movement. However, after the departure of Senator Al Song, March Fong Eu, and Assembly members Bannai and Mori, there was a gap of Asian representation in the California Legislature. This was the period when the Senate created the Senate Office of Asian Pacific Affairs giving Georgette and me the opportunity to fill the void of Asian legislative representation in the State Capitol.

When the new wave of APIA legislators was elected in the mid-1980s to early1990s, chairs of the APIA Legislative Caucus, Mike Honda, Judy Chu, and Alberto Torrico were the most dedicated in trying to raise the influence of APIA political voice in the state Capitol to a new level.

Today, Georgette and I experience the greatest satisfaction in seeing the progress of the political empowerment of the APIA in the California Legislature.

Here in California, the APIA Legislative Caucus is the second largest in the Capitol. The 2018 elections resulted in the largest class of APIA legislators ever to serve, totaling 16, and two Asian women holding top statewide elected offices, Betty Yee, State Controller, and Fiona Ma, State Treasurer, plus John Chiang, who made a significant impact in California's primary campaign, running, albeit unsuccessfully, for governor.

...

Georgette Imura, Senate Office of APIA Affairs

GAINING A VOICE IN
DEMOCRATIC POLITICS

In the 1980s, as Georgette and I went around the state encouraging APIA candidates with leadership skills to seek public office, we realized that in order to win elected offices, APIA candidates needed to participate in state party politics. We knew that candidates endorsed by their state party system receive grass roots support and financial resources to help them win.

Georgette and I were able to attend our first Democratic state party convention as alternate delegates in 1980. The vice chair of the California Democratic Party at that time was Tom Hsieh, a prominent Chinese American Democratic political figure from San Francisco, who knew us by reputation and encouraged us to help the newly established APIA Caucus of the California Democratic Party.

This particular year, the election of the state chair of the APIA Caucus was extremely contentious between two rival Asian Democratic clubs in San Francisco. Jeff Mori, representing the San Francisco Japanese American Democratic Club, was running against Jim Sing, representing the San Francisco Chinese American Democratic Club.

This caucus election was the buzz of the convention because both sides were busing in people from the Bay Area to register to vote for each candidate. APIA Caucus delegates who represented areas outside of the Bay Area were extremely concerned that the divisive aftermath of this election would be harmful to the growth of this new young caucus and were seeking a unifying compromise slate of candidates.

Georgette and I were well established statewide through our Asian Legislative Staff Caucus efforts, so we were drafted to serve as the compromise slate. We left our very first state Democratic Party convention with me serving as the chair of the California Democratic Party APIA Caucus and Georgette serving as the Northern California vice chair. Collin Lai, who led the effort to run a compromise team, was elected Southern California vice chair. Also elected was Berkeley activist Ying Lee Kelley as secretary; San Francisco Chinese Democratic Club leader Wilson Chang as treasurer; and Fely Horanzy, northern secretary; and Glenn Barroga, southern secretary, representing San Diego.

...

The organization of the first California Asian Pacific State Democratic Leadership Conference took place February 12-14, 1982, in Sacramento, California

In 1981, as newly elected officers of the APIA Caucus of the CDP, Georgette and I inherited a statewide network of dedicated grassroots APIA Democrats who were interested in recruiting more members into the Democratic Party. At the time, the APIA voter base was equally split between the Democrats and Republicans and, because the voting bloc was miniscule compared to African American and Latino numbers, the split between the two parties further diluted the political influence of the APIA communities. In essence, APIA numbers were so small that both Republicans and Democrats ignored us.

However, Republicans were doing a better job of attracting voters because most new Asian immigrants fled to the U.S. to escape communism and the Republicans were seen as anti-communist. Secondly, many first-generation APIA valued the entrepreneurial spirit and were small business owners who felt more in tune with the Republican Party. Thirdly, Japanese Americans remembered it was a Democratic president, Franklin D. Roosevelt, who signed the order for the incarceration of 120,000 Japanese Americans during World War II.

Those of us who were Democrats strongly believed that our party was more open to diversity and equal opportunity and fighting discrimination and civil rights issues that were plaguing our communities. However, both major parties were equally guilty of only giving the APIA voters lip service during this era while the APIA community itself was guilty of not demanding more.

Georgette and I felt it was time for our APIA's to gain some political attention within the California State Democratic Party.

It was hard for our community to compete with Cesar Chavez's farmworker movement, which was galvanizing the political voice of Latinos; and it was even more difficult to compete with the Martin Luther King-inspired civil rights movement of the African Americans.

With a network of the APIA state party delegates and the local APIA Democratic clubs around the state, Georgette and I felt we had the capability of putting together a statewide forum to provide exposure to gubernatorial candidates who wanted to address the multi-ethnic leadership of the APIA Democratic voter base and define what value the APIA vote could provide to key district campaigns.

And so, in 1982, we launched the first statewide APIA Democratic Leadership Conference.

The caucus's executive team worked for six months to bring together APIA Democratic leaders from every major sub-ethnic group in different parts of the state. This was not an easy task because each group was fighting for individual recognition.

Our task was to convince these sub-ethnic APIA leaders that we were stronger in numbers speaking with one voice as Asian Pacific Islanders Americans, and the conference represented that historic moment of uniting all these sub-ethnic groups—Japanese, Chinese, Korean, Filipino, Vietnamese, and South Asian—under one roof. This was why we added the word "United" to the conference title.

Honorary elected co-sponsors of this historic California event included March Fong Eu, Norm Mineta, Bob Matsui, David Roberti, and Willie L. Brown Jr. But the person who helped bring legitimacy to our statewide conference was U.S. Senator Alan Cranston, who agreed to deliver the keynote address, thanks to the encouragement of Jadine Nielsen, who was one of the most effective Asian American staff managers in the U.S. Senate at that time.

At the conference, the late mayor of Los Angeles, Tom Bradley, became the first Democratic candidate for governor to address a statewide audience of APIA Democratic leaders.

Georgette and I personally solicited contributions from elected officials we identified as close to the APIA communities. The theme of the conference was, "The United Winning Margin," which helped define the role of the APIA voter base. The message was to emphasize that, while the APIA voters' base was comparatively small, it was large enough in key districts to make a difference in close races and had the capacity to provide the winning margin for close state constitutional races.

How did we prove it? The Assembly Democratic caucus provided us with data that showed 10 percent of California's congressional districts had an APIA voter base of 5% or more because of the fast growth of Asian immigrants entering California. The conference demonstrated that the APIA community's fundraising prowess, combined with the growing numbers of the APIA voter base in key districts and elections, was a wakeup call to California's political establishment who were finally realizing the political value of the APIA community as a whole.

In addition to our hard-working Caucus officers, the conference committee and participants truly represented the grass roots trailblazers of this era when the APIA role in politics was in its infancy. To this day many of these Asian American torchbearers of California politics have left a legacy for this generation of leaders to follow. (See acknowledgement in the appendix)

...

The National APIA Democratic Conference for U.S. presidential candidates addressed APIA issues before a unified public forum for the first time in history in 1987.

The 1982 statewide conference caught the interest of Ginger Lew, a young, well-known Asian American woman in Washington D.C. circles who was the first Chinese American to be appointed to a senior policy position as Deputy Assistant Secretary during the Carter administration. She broke the glass ceiling for APIA in the nation's capital and used her influence to encourage more APIA to participate in government and politics at the national level.

In 1985, The Democratic National Committee (DNC) came under fire when the new chair, Paul Kirk, dismantled a number of special interest caucuses for the sake of unifying the party under "one tent" versus many special interest caucuses. The newest caucuses yet to be chartered were immediately dismantled and this included the Asian Pacific Islander Caucus.

There was a backlash from loyal APIA Democratic leaders from states who felt that, once again, their communities were being ignored and disrespected by the Democratic Party and were threatening to leave, while at the same time the Republican Party was strongly courting members of the APIA community.

I received a call from Ginger, who was asked by Chairman Kirk if she could start an auxiliary Asian Democratic organization that would be partially funded by the DNC, called the National Democratic Council of Asian Pacific Americans (NDCAPA) to appease the disgruntled APIA democratic base. However, when Ginger's husband was offered a new position in Paris, she asked if I could help launch the Council by organizing a national conference of APIA Democrats using the same methodology and approach I used to organize the APIA democrats in California, but this time nationally.

Ginger had already selected an executive director, Susan Lee, who was based in Washington, to help me co-ordinate the fundraising and outreach to states outside of California. (Susan subsequently became a state representative in the state of Virginia).

Ginger and Susan had secured seed funding for this national convention from the Democratic National Committee and the American Federation of State, County and Municipal Employees (AFSCME,) which was facilitated by Gloria Caiole, the special assistant to AFSCME president Gerald McEntee.

But it would be up to Susan Lee and me to secure the remaining funding for a year prior to the 1988 presidential election. Ginger, as the founding Chair of NDCAPA, would be responsible for working the D.C. political network to secure the appearance of the presidential candidates. The goal of the conference was to provide presidential candidates a public forum to address APIA issues for the first time in history.

Fortunately, my position with the Senate Office of Asian Pacific Affairs gave me a network and a title to undertake this enormous project. My boss, Senator Roberti, also understood the high stakes in protecting the APIA Democratic voter base, which was why he encouraged me to proceed, with the understanding I would have to conduct NDCAPA business on my own time.

I knew I needed a Southern California APIA leader to help me conduct a statewide fundraising effort. I asked Barbara Miyamoto, a highly respected Asian American senior staff person with then L.A. City Councilman Mike Woo, to co-chair the NDCAPA conference. Barbara, a popular political figure in Southern California, had an impeccable reputation for getting things done.

The convention location would be in Los Angeles, Oct. 16–18, 1987. Barbara and I spent one and a half years traveling around the state and to Washington D.C. to meet with congress members and contacted APIA Democratic leaders in key states such as Hawaii, Michigan, New York, Texas, and Illinois to promote the event.

While Susan Lee was busy courting institutional funders, Barbara and I stunned the traditional APIA Democrats when we proposed to turn the tables on congressional members who were accustomed to asking the APIA community for contributions and ask them to return the favor by funding this historic convention.

Thanks to the assistance of Bob Matsui, Norman Mineta, and personal friends in Congress such as Nancy Pelosi, Phil Burton, Vic Fazio, Howard Berman, Mel Levine, and Julian Dixon, whose calls to colleagues opened doors for Barbara and me to secure funding from 22 congressional members, including the House and Senate leadership. Additional funding came from the state legislators led by Pres. pro tem Roberti, Speaker Brown, as well as the state constitutional officers led by Secretary of State March Fong Eu.

Our most daunting task was giving as many APIA Democratic grassroots leaders a role in this historic undertaking by creating three regional steering committees (Los Angeles, Northern California, and Washington D.C) and convening a diverse interim Board of Directors representing sub-ethnic APIA groups from diverse regions. Approximately 150 national APIA leaders played a role in organizing this seminal conference and helped make history.

. . .

Without the blood, sweat, and tears of all these participants, who believed in this dream, this convention would never have happened. (See acknowledgement in the appendix). As each of the presidential candidates (Governor Michael Dukakis, Reverend Jesse Jackson, and Senator Paul Simon) walked on stage to explain why they cared about APIA issues and APIA voters, I saw the look of pride and gratitude on the face of each APIA contributor to this convention. It was history in action.

As for Ginger, Barbara, and me, we live with the satisfaction of knowing that our APIA community was finally being acknowledged as an equal to other diverse communities. As noted in the event program:

"This convention is making the statement that the Asian Pacific Islander American Democratic voters will no longer tolerate being ignored, unrecognized, or silent. This national convention marks the beginning of a tradition which will require future leaders of our country to be prepared to address our issues as well as recognize our efforts and commitment toward the goals of the Democratic Party."

. . .

From top to bottom: Celebrating the first National APIA Democratic Conference in 1988. Presidential candidate Michael Dukakis, Barbara Miyamoto, Susan Lee, Ambassador Linda Tsao Yang; Mayor Tom Bradley at "United Winning Margin" 1982 conference; Presidential candidate Michael Dukakis

THE RISE OF A NATIONAL AGENDA

The successful 1987 convention of the National Democratic Council of Asian Pacific Americans (NDCAPA) helped to pave the road for the national Asian voter base to play more prominent roles in presidential politics as exemplified by the campaigns of Jesse Jackson, George Bush, and Michael Dukakis. Jackson's campaign team was led by the first Asian American to manage a presidential campaign, Eddie Wong. Both the Bush and Dukakis campaigns made a concerted effort to recruit APIA into their campaigns and there was more APIA representation at both the Republican and Democratic national conventions.

Many organizers of the NDCAPA convention, including yours truly, were selected to be delegates at the Atlanta Democratic National Convention with leadership roles on the convention floor. Thirty- eight APIA delegates were appointed from the state of California alone, representing 10 percent of the state's population.

Over 100 APIA delegates gathered at the 1988 Atlanta Democratic Convention. It was immediately noted that all the special interest and ethnic minority delegations had specified program agendas, with the exception of the APIA delegation. To help fill this remarkable void, a group of delegates including Irene Natividad, a noted female activist from Washington D.C.,

Jim Shimoura from Detroit, Ross Harano from Chicago, Lani Sakoda from Hawaii, and Ginger Lew, Barbara Miyamoto, Susan Lee, Jadine Nielsen, Gloria Caiole, Eddie Wong, and Mable Teng from the Rainbow Coalition collaborated to put together a last-minute program agenda for the APIA convention delegates. The group was assisted by an energetic and dedicated volunteer, Janie Fong, a recent UCLA grad who also helped with the NDCAPA conference. Janie eventually became California's Hong Kong trade representative and is now an executive with the East West Bank in Hong Kong.

With no official affiliation with the DNC, we had to quickly find a corporate sponsor for our signature reception event, fight for last minute meeting spaces close by the convention, and form our own means of communication among all the APIA delegates. I begged one of my California lobbyist friends, Rick Melendez with Atlantic Richfield Oil Company (ARCO), a convention sponsor, to see if he could get ARCO to help us fund a reception. Once ARCO agreed, Gloria Caiole with the AFSCME union once again came through to supplement ARCO's funding, enabling us to host a convention wide brunch event.

Our second challenge was getting a top name as our special guest to give stature to our convention event. Thanks to the strong arm-twisting of Congress members Mineta, Matsui, and Senator Inouye, we were able to get the candidate's wife, Kitty Dukakis, to fill this role.

Our event was so last-minute we were only able to find a Chinese restaurant in a small shopping mall close by the convention to hold our event. With so much competition from other events on the calendar, we were not sure how many delegates would attend. Little did we know that we would get an overflow of convention delegates yearning for some good Chinese food instead of the standard convention party fare.

Looking back, this convention was a historic recognition that APIA voters deserve to be part of the voice of the Democratic National Party. Four years later, the APIA Caucus became part of the Democratic National Committee Convention structure and this was the last time APIA delegates were left on their own to fight for a piece of attention at the presidential conventions. This became my formal introduction to national party politics.

...

After the NDCAPA conference and my work at the national convention, I was identified as one of the national Democratic APIA leaders. Senator Roberti was asked by Dukakis' California campaign if he would loan me and another Roberti staffer, Cindy Lavagetto, a prominent campaign consultant, to the California presidential campaign. The campaign told Roberti that I would be designated as a deputy director of the California campaign.

This assignment meant I had to leave my family for a few months to work out of the L.A. headquarters. Luckily, Cindy and I had been friends for years, so we decided to room together in a barely furnished condo in Hancock Park provided pro bono by fundraiser Maria Hsia, who was supporting the Dukakis campaign.

I quickly found that working on a presidential campaign is like being in a 24/7 whirlwind, constantly putting out fires while trying to be creative on how to handle the demands of the all the constituency groups of the largest state in the nation so that they would all feel special.

The campaign executive team was headed by Tony Podesta (brother of Clinton's former chief of staff, John Podesta), honorary chair Ron Brown, campaign director Kathy Garmezy, and press secretary Dede Meyers, who later became press secretary to President Clinton. I was also excited that my close friend, Ron Wakabayashi, former executive director of JACL, was also recruited to help with the grassroots community efforts along with two additional APIA, Steve Arevalo and Marissa Castro.

Many times, I felt out of my league, because I did not have the campaign expertise working a presidential campaign among some of the best campaign minds in the country.

But it was the first time the APIA constituency base in California had one of their own in an executive position of a presidential campaign. The demands from the many APIA sub-ethnic groups were challenging, making sure each group received their fair share of attention from the campaign.

The sharp-minded Garmezy quickly realized that my relationships with 120 state legislators in California made me the ideal trouble shooter between the campaign and the state legislature. This meant I had to make sure every Democratic elected official was included whenever Dukakis made an appearance in their districts.

Toward the waning days of the campaign, the TV ad with Dukakis wearing the silly helmet in an army tank, coupled with the Willie Horton ads, and Dukakis' poor debate performance, seriously eroded his standing in the polls. Those last days were unforgettable as I saw a brave campaign team continue to fight for every single vote, even though the polls around the country signaled that we were in for a landslide defeat.

On election night, I remember the faces of our campaign team as we watched the devastating election results favoring Bush. Still, the California team took great pride in the fact that Dukakis did the best in California, losing the state to Bush by the smallest margin.

I had no regrets because it was an honor to work for such a respectable, intelligent, and gracious candidate.

However, this would be the last time I accepted a paid position with a presidential campaign, because my time away from home during this time almost cost me my marriage. During the last days of the campaign, my husband Ron was going through the grief of losing his brother Ken to cancer. He needed me to be there for him during Ken's last days, but because I was in charge of Dukakis' last major campaign event in San Francisco, Chinatown, I felt I couldn't leave the campaign.

It took a long time for Ron to forgive me for making such a heartless choice.

...

After the Dukakis campaign, I received a call from L.A. attorney Johnnie Cochran, who later gained fame as O.J. Simpson's attorney. I met Johnnie during the Dukakis campaign. He and Ron Brown wanted to meet with me in Los Angeles to discuss APIA politics in California, and I asked Barbara Miyamoto, the co-chair of NDCAPA, to join me at the meeting at the Biltmore Hotel.

Ron Brown, whom I had met during the California Dukakis campaign, was a powerful African American figure in Washington D.C. After leading the national Urban League, he had become a top campaign and congressional aide to Sen. Ted Kennedy before becoming a prominent lobbyist with the most prestigious Washington law and lobbying firm, Patton Boggs.

Johnnie Cochran was there to advocate for Ron Brown's candidacy to serve as Chair of the Democratic National Committee (DNC). Ron indicated the DNC needed new energy and he wanted his administration to be a rainbow coalition, but he needed help in getting the APIA support for his candidacy. Barbara and I asked Ron point blank if he would reinstate the DNC Asian Pacific Islander caucus.

He surprised us by saying no. "I won't be able to fulfill that promise because the southern caucus of the DNC was against all the small diversified special interest caucuses," he said. Bottom line: Ron could not win the chairmanship without this region's support. But Ron hastily promised that he would find ways to empower the APIA voice within the DNC as well as hire APIA staff to work in his administration.

Both Barbara and I were struck by Ron's candor, and our gut told us that if he was honest enough to say no to us, he would fulfill his commitment to ensure APIA would have more of a voice and presence with the DNC under his chairmanship. With that commitment in mind, I first sought the counsel of Mineta and Matsui. Then I made calls to APIA political leaders who worked with me during the NDCAPA national convention and discussed Ron's commitment to the APIA constituency if he was elected chair. I was fortunate that many of the APIA Democratic Party activists trusted me and allowed Ron Brown to use their names as a part of his support base, showing a unified rainbow coalition of support.

As soon as Ron Brown was elected DNC chair, he asked me for names of APIA candidates to serve in his administration. One of the names I recommended was Melinda Yee, who was on staff with the National Organization of Chinese Americans at the time. She nailed her interview and eventually became an integral part of Ron Brown's DNC staff as well as his Commerce staff when he became Secretary of Commerce.

...

A few months after Ron Brown's election, during a dinner in San Francisco's Chinatown, Congressman Mineta came up to me and said, "Hey, congratulations. I understand that you'll be appointed to the DNC executive committee, which is exciting news because we need more Asian Americans at the head table, Maeley."

I was completely surprised by his comment until I received a call from Ron Brown within the next few days telling me he wanted me to serve on the executive committee of the DNC. Before I agreed to serve on the DNC executive committee, I asked Chairman Brown how he was going to fulfill his commitment to Asian Pacific Democrats.

It was a question I never had to ask again.

He was so excited to tell me that he was going to make Congressman Matsui treasurer of the DNC, making him the first Asian American to serve as an officer of the Democratic Party. He reminded me that I would be the first non-elected Asian American to serve on the DNC executive committee. He immediately asked Melinda Yee to help launch an unprecedented aggressive national APIA outreach program and made sure there was APIA staff, such as Sharon Ynagi, included in policy, research, and other strategic political positions.

When I accepted the DNC appointment, I did not realize the time and expense this appointment required. Meetings were held in different states and DNC members had to pay for their own travel and accommodation expenses

The first regional meeting was in Minneapolis. I arrived on a midnight flight and cabs were scarce at the airport during that hour. I finally was able to hail a cab driving toward me when, suddenly, a white man dashed into the cab ahead of me. I walked to the cab and told the driver I was sure he was coming for me. The driver nodded that he was but, with the man in the cab, the driver said, "Why don't you get in and I'll get you both to your destinations."

The man looked at me closely under the streetlight and said, "I don't want to share a cab with her kind."

The driver told the guy, "Ok, you get out, because she's going to be my passenger."

I thanked the white male driver profusely but was stunned by the incident because it had been so long since I was a victim of racist behavior by a stranger. I had forgotten how it felt. This was not a good beginning to my start with the DNC executive committee.

During my first meeting, I realized the executive committee was composed of elected members of state and federal offices, high ranking party officials, and high-profile representatives from ethnic groups and labor.

While the California members of the executive committee, including Congresswoman Maxine Waters, welcomed me warmly, I found the other executive committee members from the other states were not very welcoming and preferred to stay within their own cliques. Perhaps it was because I was not an elected official or a celebrity of any sorts. I was simply a non-elected Asian serving on the executive committee representing the APIA constituency.

I learned that the turnover rate of executive committee member appointments was extremely low. Belonging to this committee was like belonging to an exclusive elitist club with lifetime benefits such as serving as super delegates at the National convention and being invited to all the "A" list special events at the convention.

During the public DNC executive committee meetings, which took place before hundreds of elected members of the Democratic National Committee, I was usually the only Asian sitting on the stage platform. Matsui was so busy with his leadership role in Congress, he rarely attended the regional DNC executive committee meetings.

It took me a while to find my voice. With so many experienced special interest leaders and office holders sitting on the executive committee stage platform, people had to fight for airtime.

I wanted to contribute to the discussion, but hesitated from the fear I'd say something wrong, as I was not totally aware of the rules of protocol. When I finally found the courage to speak, I raised my hand, but was initially ignored because these high-powered executive committee members did not wait to be called and just spoke over one another with the loudest voice prevailing.

Whenever issues arose regarding diversity or ethnic politics the discussions would automatically refer to just Browns and Blacks. After being ignored time and time again, I decided I was not there to be window dressing. I forced myself to interject into the discussion by raising my hand, waiting for a quick pause, then raising my voice as loud as I could, saying, "Excuse me, but I would like to be heard on this issue."

The first time I did this, I saw by the reaction of the executive committee members that they were unaccustomed to having an

Asian who was not an elected official aggressively assert herself into public discussions. But, as my self-confidence grew in expressing myself publicly before this body of the nation's leading Democrats, so did the committee's respect for what I had to say.

. . .

When Ron Brown received the invitation to become the first chairman of the Democratic Party to visit Taiwan, he asked Melinda Yee and me to join him on this trip. Even though he kidded Melinda and me for not being good translators, he said we at least "looked the look and walked the walk."

Melinda and I were so proud to staff Ron Brown on this trip because he was such a charismatic representative for the U.S. Democratic Party. There was only one occasion when he asked for my advice about addressing a group of China's top industrialists at a private dinner in Hong Kong. I told him that the Chinese are so used to the U.S. constantly lecturing them about the U.S., why not try a different approach and "tell them that you are there to listen and learn from them about their economic successes."

This approach was so refreshing and appreciated by the host of Chinese executives. One could see how impressed they were as he went around the table to listen to each of them speak. In short, he was giving them "face," which is important in the Asian culture.

But, being a human rights activist, Brown could not help himself but to inject his opinion about the need for China to reform its human rights practices. Sitting next to me was Stanley Fong, one of the world's largest jade exporters, who said through a translator: "The U.S. needs to be careful about making human rights a condition in doing business with China. China has now enabled every person to enjoy a bowl of rice and that is more important than human rights at this time. Trying to demean China about human rights will not help, because China would rather give up the country than lose face before the world."

As we were waiting for the car, Ron proudly asked me how he did. I told him he was great until he injected the human rights lecture to these pro-China industrialists. And I informed him that I was amused the translator graciously covered over Mr. Fong's real statement in Cantonese which became, "When you have a country fighting to give every person a bowl of rice, you can just 'screw' human rights."

I believe Stanley Fong's advice stayed with Ron because, when he became Commerce Secretary, Brown championed the much-debated idea that instead of making human rights a condition for commercial engagement, commercial engagement should take place between China and the U.S. as an incentive for China to improve its human rights practices.

...

At the start of the 1992 presidential campaign, the Democrats were touting seven potential presidential candidates, including one of my favorites, Paul Simon, who had a large Asian base in Chicago.

During the California primary, the state party, headed by Phil Angelides, was hosting a breakfast featuring all seven candidates. I was going to attend with Maria Hsia, who by now was a high-profile influential donor to the California Democratic Party. But at the last minute she told me to attend without her, which caused me to be late. When I arrived, there was a seat at the Bill Clinton table probably saved for Maria Hsia. Angelides did not want an empty seat at this table, so he directed me to sit next to Clinton. The candidates were already on stage. I was relieved to see friends like former Assembly Majority Leader Mike Roos and attorney Johnnie Cochran also seated at this table.

After the presentations, Gov. Clinton returned to the table and introduced himself to me. Roos was very gracious to give Clinton information about my background. Clinton proceeded to go around the table asking each guest to give him feedback on what they thought of his speech. Everyone was generous with their accolades because Clinton is such a charismatic speaker.

Since I was so busy eating my breakfast, I was only half-paying attention. I was hoping he would not ask me because I came in late. But, when it came to my turn, I tried to concentrate on my scrambled eggs and avoid eye contact so he would skip me. But my mischievous friend Cochran yelled across the table, "Maeley, he's waiting for you to tell him what you thought of his speech." Clinton looked at me with that big smile and quietly waited for me to finish the food in my mouth, so I knew I had to speak.

I told him that I thought he started out great and piqued my interest with a story about his conversation with a taxi driver asking him about his dreams of success in America. But then I said, "You rambled on so long that I lost you because you didn't leave me with a sound bite at the end."

The table went silent, but Johnnie Cochran loved it and gave me a quick wink of approval. I did not know what reaction I would get from Clinton, but he gave his famous chuckle, throwing his head back, and said without a moment's hesitation, "I need you to help me with my campaign." He was so smooth and clever that I immediately wanted to say yes.

I knew nothing about him except his speech during the national convention in Atlanta, so I asked him, "How familiar are you with Asian Pacific issues in this country?" His immediate response was, "I have a remarkable Filipina woman serving on my cabinet, Maria Haley, who serves as a reference for me regarding Asian issues, but I can always use your help to learn more about your community's issues."

With that, we exchanged cards. As impressed as I was with Clinton, I was still leaning toward Simon.

Months later, with the presidential campaign in full swing, instead of putting together another national APIA Democratic leadership conference, Congressmen Matsui and Mineta convened an APIA Democratic leadership meeting in Washington for selected APIA leaders around the country to meet with Clinton. The round-table discussion allowed leading APIA Democrats to ask Clinton his positions on issues as well as provide him a chance to discuss why he wanted to be president. At the end of the discussion, we all lined up to take photos and chat with Clinton personally. When Clinton saw me, he did not recall my name, but he pointed to me and said "Breakfast, LA. So glad you are here."

He almost won me over that moment with his amazing memory. But I remained uncommitted because I wasn't sure he would be able to overcome the scandals that were surfacing, until Ron Brown convinced me that Clinton would ultimately win the election. I trusted Ron's political acumen as much as Ron trusted my leadership role with the Asian American voter base. So, when he asked me to help the Clinton campaign, it was hard to say no.

...

When Clinton/Gore secured the nomination at the national Democratic convention there were more APIA delegates than ever before.

The National Council of Asian Pacific American (NDCAPA) efforts during the 1988 Democratic convention in Atlanta helped provide the permanent inclusion of APIA convention activities as a formal part of the Democratic National Convention program.

Clinton had a much wider base of support among APIA voters than Dukakis because of the early backing he received from Congress members Matsui and Mineta, and the campaign had a talented APIA team in Washington D.C., headed by his former Arkansas cabinet member Maria Haley, and Irene Bueno, a well-known political consultant in Washington D.C., among others. The campaign aggressively courted the APIA voter base, and it paid off. This voter base was now trending more in support of Democrats versus Republicans.

Helping Clinton, as a volunteer, during his presidential campaign with advance logistics for his California APIA appearances was like being with a rock star. He was easy to work with and people loved his magnetic personality. I found his ability to connect with any type of audience to be remarkable. The way he digested last-minute talking points and interjected these points into the speech was brilliant.

I found Gore to be personal, warm, and charming in a private conversational setting, but he seemed to struggle in conveying that same warmth and charm in a large public setting. I feel so fortunate to have had the chance to help with the Clinton/Gore campaigns and will always appreciate how respectful and responsive both candidates were to the staff working with them. But, the greatest reward of this experience was enjoying the sweet victory of this presidential campaign.

...

Unfortunately, while serving as Commerce Secretary during the Clinton administration, Ron Brown died in a plane crash April 3, 1996, near Dubrovnik, Croatia, leading a delegation of CEO's on a trade mission.

His sudden death was so devastating to me because of the friendship we shared during his years as the DNC chair. I sadly wrote an editorial tribute to Ron Brown in the April 12, 1996, edition of *Asian Week*, "Honoring a consummate advocate for Asian Pacific Americans."

...

The learning experiences I had working in national politics and presidential campaigns were unforgettable, along with the thrill of being able to contribute to the success of a presidential campaign. But the one major lesson in life that I learned is that nothing, not even presidential politics, should ever take precedence over family priorities. This why I never worked another presidential campaign that mandated living away from my family ever again.

President Clinton at the White House; Kitty Dukakis, special guest at Atlanta DNC convention; Delegate at the 1987 Democratic National Convention; Super Delegate at the 1995 Democratic National Convention

BOOK FOUR

Scandal...

"We have learned certain lessons. We have learned not to be neutral in times of crisis for neutrality always helps the aggressor, never the victim. We have learned that silence is never the answer. Above all we have learned that indifference to evil is an evil in and of itself"
—Elie Wiesel

THE ASIAN CAMPAIGN
FINANCE SCANDAL

After the 1996 elections, *New York Times* articles by William Safire and other journalists were surfacing, with stories of large donations to the Democratic Party during the Clinton re-election campaign coming from Asian foreign nationals. I was in Cancun on vacation when I picked up a *USA Today* and saw the names of Maria Hsia, John Huang, and James Riady, alleging their involvement in an illegal fundraising scheme.

I was absolutely shocked to see my friends' names being maligned on the front page of a national newspaper. I was sure it was a misunderstanding inflamed by the fact that Asian Americans are always portrayed as foreigners.

At this time, I was serving on the DNC executive committee and John Huang was an appointed vice chair. I was a visible figure at all the presidential Asian American sponsored fundraising events managed by Vice Chair John Huang because of my status with the DNC, and I interacted with many of the named donors during the Clinton presidential campaign. John would also generously comp a number of Asian American community leaders who did not have the resources to attend these high donor events so they, too, would have the opportunity to have face time with the President and Vice president.

Initially, I thought the Asian campaign fundraising allegations would be a momentary headline and never imagined that the story would have "legs," as they say in politics. But as the news headlines proliferated, I became nervous and decided it was best to terminate my contract with Lippo in case it was misconstrued that I was a fundraiser on contract. Luckily, as part of my consulting contract, I provided monthly reports of my political and community activities with billing statements.

But unfortunately, as the media dug deeper into the huge checks being written by strange Asian-surname donors, more questions arose regarding their resident status and business backgrounds here in the U.S. This raised a red flag that led to a Senate investigation into the legality of a number of other big Asian-surname donor checks.

As a result of the investigation of the $3.4 million dollars raised by John Huang during this period, the DNC returned $1.2 million of checks that were not appropriately vetted. They found that some of these funds improperly came from foreign companies or from individuals who were not living in the U.S. legally or were not American citizens.

But the fundraising event that attracted the most media attention was the Hsi Lai Temple event in Hacienda Heights, California, for Vice President Gore, where Buddhist Temple nuns were found to be used as straw donors for the event.

In April 1996, John Huang called to ask if I could travel to Los Angeles and stay over at his house to help him and his wife Jane handle logistics for an event for Vice President Gore in Monterey Park. The evening before the event I could tell that John and Maria Hsia were having heated telephone discussions about schedule conflicts over Gore's appearance.

Huang's plan was to have a fundraiser at a Monterey Park restaurant, but that would conflict with Maria's commitment for

Gore to appear at the Hsi Lai Temple, an organization that was very close to Maria. I am not sure how the decision was made to combine the two events. I know John was quite upset over sending fundraising donors from the restaurant to meet Gore at the Temple.

At the Temple, I watched Gore's entrance, waving to the people on the balcony, and then it was my turn to greet and escort attendees to their assigned tables. I remember chatting with Congressman Bob Matsui, who introduced Gore at the event. By this time, I was not sure if this was a fundraising event or a public event because I did not see anyone collecting checks. After the luncheon, there were photo ops with Gore in front of the Temple's emblem. To me, this was just another Clinton/Gore event with the APIA community.

...

As more press stories circulated about the Democratic National Committee (DNC) receiving illegal foreign donations, allegedly being financed by China to influence U.S. politics, I became extremely concerned. Would I be dragged into this scandal because of my association with many of the figures involved, my contract with Lippo, and my attendance at the fundraising events noted by the press?

And sure enough, as my name started to surface in the media, I became paranoid that my association with Huang and others would be a liability to Cassidy & Associates. It was not uncommon for major lobbying firms in D.C. to terminate any association with staff who attract negative publicity to the firm. Congressman Vic Fazio even cautioned me to expect that my association with this scandal could hurt my employment with such a prominent firm as Cassidy and Associates.

I decided to meet with Gerry Cassidy to discuss my predicament as he was aware of my association with all Asian American events associated with Pres. Clinton or Vice President Gore. To my surprise, Cassidy calmly told me that he had no intention of letting me go. Instead, he told me to lie low in California for a while. He would have Cassidy's public relations team headed by Jody Powell handle any press inquiries. Dale Liebach and Brent Gilroy were assigned to be my personal handlers during this crisis. Cassidy also suggested that I would need to "lawyer up." I was relieved and touched by his kindness, understanding, and willingness to stand by me during this crisis.

Mark Cowan, who had brought me into the firm, advised me that I needed to get a Washington D.C. attorney who specializes in these cases; these attorneys knew the culture, the players, and the thinking of a Washington-driven investigation. I turned to one of the most highly respected Asian attorneys in the country, my long-time close friend, Dale Minami, for advice .

Dale gained national fame as one of the lead attorneys among a young team of pro bono lawyers who succeeded in overturning the conviction of Fred Korematsu, whose defiance of the World War II Japanese American Internment order lead to Korematsu v. United States, one of the most controversial United States Supreme Court decisions of the 20th century. Dale's civil rights and legal accomplishments made him an icon within the APIA community as well as the legal community. In 2003, he received the Thurgood Marshall Award from the American Bar Association and most recently became the first Asian American attorney to receive the distinguished American Bar Association's medal in its 90-year history.

Dale agreed that a Washington D.C. attorney would be my best option. But, typical of Dale's generosity, he offered to help with my case because he was based here in California with me. I also sought the advice of Jerry Chong, one of the best criminal lawyers in Sacramento. He was so angry about the racist manner in which the media was handling this issue. He told me that if I ever needed legal help in Sacramento, he also would be available to help me pro bono. I didn't realize at the time how lucky I was to have both Dale Minami and Jerry Chong in my corner.

Melinda Yee was already facing allegations associated with illegal fundraising during her days at the Department of Commerce, working with Ron Brown.

...

During the Clinton years, Melinda and I remained close and attended many of John Huang's events together. I was becoming concerned about Melinda, who was now working for San Francisco Mayor Willie Brown, because she was taking such a beating in the press. She, too, was forced to hire an attorney on her own and create a legal defense fund to help defray costs.

This really frightened me because I had not thought about legal fees, should I become publicly entangled in this growing scandal.

Melinda told me she initially was going to hire the late Ron Brown's former attorney, the very high-profile Reid Weingarten. Weingarten was already representing one of the major Asian figures being targeted by the committee, the wealthy Thai businesswoman, Pauline Kanchanalak.

Weingarten referred Melinda to his friend and colleague, Nancy Luque, who had been named one of Washington's 100 top lawyers and was a former federal prosecutor who knew the system inside and out. One of Nancy's high-profile clients was Congressman Dan Rostenkowski, the former Democratic leader in Congress.

Melinda was so happy with her attorney, she highly recommended her to me.

When I approached Nancy about my situation, we immediately connected. I was so impressed with her knowledge, confidence, empathy and compassion. She was tough, nothing rattled her, and she was quick in responding to allegations and innuendoes. She became my strength and anchor through the ordeal I was about to face.

...

On May 12, my name surfaced in a *Wall Street Journal* article with the headline, "Asian Political Money Flowed in California Before D.C. Found It," detailing the growing influence of the Pacific Leadership Fund (PLF) PAC headed by Maria Hsia and John Huang. I was named as one of the founders and as the link between this PAC and Asian American politics. The article disclosed my close relationship with John Huang.

It was important that I quickly dispute my portrayal as a fundraiser or a founder of the Pacific Leadership Fund. I made a call to then-retired Lt. Governor Leo McCarthy who was associated with the start of the Pacific Leadership Fund PAC through his friendship with Maria Hsia. I asked if he would write a correction to the *Wall Street Journal* indicating that I was never a part of the Pacific Leadership Fund PAC. Leo instantly agreed and sent a note to the *Wall Street Journal* with that statement. Leo also tried to be as comforting as possible during this time, sensing how much duress I was under and probably understanding there was more to come.

I felt even worse about how my notoriety was affecting Cassidy and Associates, as articles tried to tie the scandal to the firm's lobbying activities for Taiwan. By this time the media was hungry for any stories linking Asian influence in Washington D.C. Once again, Gerry Cassidy told me not to worry and to let Powell/Tate, the firm's public relations arm, handle this issue.

. . .

All my Asian American friends who were in any position of power within the Clinton administration were being dragged into the media frenzy, starting with an article on Bob and Doris Matsui because of Doris' position as a public liaison in the White House, and Congressman Bob Matsui's role as the deputy chairman of the Democratic National Committee. With the help of the White House, Bob and Doris Matsui quickly dispelled that they had anything to do with the fundraising scandal and distanced themselves from anything and anyone associated with the growing scandal.

One of my closest friends, Bill Kaneko from Hawaii, who did such a great job at the DNC as the APIA liaison, was now being investigated by the Dept. of Justice and Congressional oversight committees, as was another close friend, Mona Pasquil, who was part of Clinton's White House staff, to see if there was any coordination between the White House and DNC fundraising activities. This harrowing experience was so new to the three of us.

Bill and Mona were provided legal counsel as employees of the White House and the DNC. Fortunately for them, they were not intimately involved with the targeted principals like I was, so they were not subjected to the same public scrutiny. But, just being able to share our everyday traumas and daily happenings with one another provided me with some sanity and support.

After months of wild speculative rumors and conspiracy theories, the Senate Governmental Affairs Committee's hearing into alleged campaign abuses in the 1996 presidential election finally started on Tuesday, July 8th, 1997. I was shocked to receive a call from an investigator with the Senate committee notifying me that they would like me to appear before the committee. This notice started me on a spiral of paranoia and fear, having never been investigated by the federal government.

My personal physician, Dr. William Taylor, was so concerned about my sudden weight loss that he immediately referred me to a therapist to help me manage my anxiety and stress. During this time, Ron was growing extremely concerned about my mental condition and was concerned I was spiraling into depression. Despite how strong I was during my childhood challenges, this episode tore at the core of my strength and resilience.

What I didn't expect was that my greatest nightmare was still to come. Two of the major pieces of evidence the committee brought forth during the first week of hearings were my letters to John Emerson and DNC Chair David Wilhelm. Due to the language in my letter to Wilhelm, the committee wanted to prove that there was a major Democratic fundraising scheme to raise illegal foreign Asian funds from East Asian business leaders. This letter made all the national headlines. My hometown paper, *The Sacramento Bee,* had my picture on the front page with the headline "Fundraising Spotlight Lands on Sacramentan."

In the letter to the DNC Chair David Wilhelm, I suggested that the party connect with a new sub- ethnic group of Asian Americans categorized as "East Asians," such as Indonesians, Malaysians, and Thais, to cultivate a relationship to expand the DNC's Asian American voter and fundraising base. However, the wording of the letter was misconstrued to imply that I wanted to fundraise from "East Asians" who were non-citizens.

In my letter to John Emerson, who I worked with on the Clinton California campaign and who was now part of the Clinton transition team, I listed APIA candidates I was recommending for appointment to the White House and administration. John Huang was on my list of recommendations, and I made a drastic error of listing John's role in fundraising in my recommendation, which the committee pointed out in the hearing as part of a conspiracy.

And finally, the committee pointed out that Huang and I had 61 phone calls between us during the last year and a half while I was on contract with Lippo, implying I was a Lippo operative helping John with some type of foreign espionage allegations.

Now my phone was ringing off the hook with inquiries from reporters, with some newspapers even sending reporters to my house to camp at my front door. Even a staffer from Ted Koppel's *Nightline* called. I literally was paralyzed from fear and did not dare leave my house for days, feeling like a prisoner in my own home. I simply could not face the embarrassment and humiliation I was feeling. I saw my entire professional and personal reputation going down the drain and, what's more, felt the shame I was bringing to my husband Ron's family. In short, this was the first time I ever felt I had lost control of my life.

By this time, the Committee was demanding that I turn over documents including bank accounts, telephone bills, address book, calendars, financial investments and campaign contributions over a five-year period to prepare for my testimony.

· · ·

My attorney, Nancy Luque, was alarmed with the frequency my name was being brought up by the Senate Committee members, portraying me as some type of "Lippo operative," and she told me she wanted to send a letter on my behalf asking the committee to immediately allow me to testify to clear my reputation. This request would run contrary to the number of witnesses who had already fled the country or pled the 5th amendment. I would be the first witness to actually request an appearance before the committee which would raise a red flag as to why I was so eager to testify. But the thought of appearing before a Senate public hearing to be interrogated by hostile Republican senators terrified me, and it was the last thing I wanted to do voluntarily. But since I trusted my attorney completely, I consented to send the letter.

Nancy took the issue one step further by asking Senator Carl Levin (D. Michigan) on the committee to please read my letter during the hearing. Levin said, after reading the letter that Chairman Fred Thompson's statements about me were "unacceptable and inappropriate," asserting I should be allowed to appear as a witness. He added the comments, "The committee is using unjustified inferences to create a mischaracterization of Ms. Tom's activities. It is unfair to raise these inferences, but not let her reply." That legal strategy by my attorney was right on target and was helpful in neutralizing some of the damaging comments made by members of the committee about my role in the fundraising schemes.

On July 19, after two weeks of hearings, Mark Gladstone's *Los Angeles Times* article, "Fund-raising Scandal Drags an Insider into the Limelight," summarized the committee's allegations against me. Gladstone concluded his article with a description of my career in the Capitol and included David Roberti's comments about my role and reputation in California as an Asian American activist which ended the article on a positive note.

Another *Sac Bee* article surfaced on Aug. 5th by Capitol reporter Dan Smith, who was familiar with my role in the Capitol. This article dwelled on my personal history and professional background in politics with quotes from supporters and friends such as Georgette Imura, David Roberti, and David Townsend, and reviewed the allegations I was facing from the committee.

The article concluded that it was unclear as to whether I would be allowed to testify before the Senate in open hearing. But, the words of Townsend at the conclusion of the article brought tears to my eyes as he defended me with the quote, "When you haven't done anything wrong, you could be crucified on the cross of innuendo. It's tough. All Maeley has ever done, really, is be an advocate for Asian Americans."

. . .

Even though I had no interest to talk to anyone during the height of the press scrutiny, because I preferred to wallow in self-pity, I received many letters and phone calls of support from friends in the Capitol and community. To this day, I've saved every letter.

I also appreciated the many friends who wrote letters to the editor of major mainstream media defending my reputation. Friends of mine who worked in politics understood politics is a "contact" sport and the higher you go in the political ladder, the more public, vicious, and vindictive the sport becomes. But, Asian friends of ours who were apolitical were so stunned by what was happening to me publicly, they did not know how to react when they saw me. Many of these friends were raised "to not be the nail in the wood that sticks out." And in my case, I was that nail.

My buddy, Georgette Imura, quickly organized a dinner at New Canton restaurant gathering my various groups of friends from the Capitol, my neighbors, my tennis group, Roberti staff,

Assembly Rules staff, my old bosses, Lou Papan and David Roberti, and legislators like Phil Isenberg and his wife Marilyn, to surprise me and cheer up my spirits. It was such an outpouring of love and support that I completely fell apart, engulfed with gratitude, which finally helped me overcome my stupor of self-pity.

Perhaps one of the kindest gestures I encountered during this period was from Panda Express founder and Chairman Andrew Cherng. I met Andrew during the time he attended various presidential events organized by John Huang who knew Andrew from the days when John was the head of the Chinese Bankers Association in Los Angeles. When we saw one another at these events, Andrew always enjoyed discussing my personal journey into politics.

At the height of the scandal, during an Asian American event in Los Angeles, Andrew expressed concern about John and me during this ordeal. He specifically asked if this episode would harm my position with Cassidy & Associates.

When I told him how supportive and helpful Cassidy & Associates was in protecting me during this period, Andrew was extremely impressed that the firm stuck by me during this firestorm of allegations. After this discussion, Andrew told me that he wanted to offer me a contract with Cassidy and Associates to do some political work for Panda Express because he was interested in expanding Panda Express into airports, Las Vegas and shopping malls. However, I believe his true motive for offering me a contract was to demonstrate his appreciation to the firm for their support of my situation.

Through the years I worked as a consultant for the Panda Company, I saw how effective Andrew and his wife Peggy were in developing a company structure and culture that became a phenomenal success to the point that it no longer needed a political strategy to succeed. I told Andrew, "You no longer need my services," and voluntarily terminated my contract with the deepest gratitude that he helped me out when I needed it the most.

My mentor, Art Torres, who was chair of the California Democratic Party at that time reminded me sternly that I should know better than to put anything in writing that could be politically misinterpreted, an act for which I paid a heavy price. And yet, Art provided support and counsel to me and my family throughout the entire ordeal.

There were some disappointments too. One senior senator I bumped into at the Capitol who I thought was a friend saw me and said loudly, "Hey, Maeley, I thought you would be in jail by now." I don't know if he was kidding or not, but I did not appreciate his humor.

Congressman Bob Matsui, when asked by *The Sacramento Bee* if he knew me, simply identified me as a "constituent" which created a lot of consternation among the local Asian community and Capitol staff because they knew how much I respected Matsui.

However, knowing how toxic Washington D.C. can be, I understood why Matsui wanted to distance himself from anyone associated with this scandal.

Congressman Vic Fazio took the opposite approach, inviting me to lunch during one of his Sacramento visits so that we could be seen together at one of the most public restaurants around the Capitol to show his support.

Mary Hayashi, who later became an Assemblywoman, had hounded me for two years to join the board of her national APIA Women's Health Organization, but immediately after my name surfaced in the media related to this scandal, she asked her secretary to call requesting that I take a leave from the board. I simply resigned.

As the media attention surrounding my role in the campaign finance investigation was dying down, I wondered if I would ever be able to regain my reputation. Then in January of 1988, I received a letter from Mark Morodami, president of the Sacramento Asian Bar Association and renowned attorney with the Fair Political

Practice Commission in Sacramento, notifying me that I was the recipient of their 1998 community service award for my contributions to the Asian American community of Sacramento. This award from the legal community of Sacramento during this period in my professional career will always be among my most treasured. To show my deep gratitude for this award, I used this occasion to discuss my ordeal in public for the first time.

Vice Pres. Gore at the Hsi Lai Temple event; Panel discussion with John Huang and Dale Minami

FIGHTING BACK

While the media scrutiny over my role died down after August, I was still waiting to be interviewed by congressional committee investigators, and my attorney was also notified that I might have to go before a Grand Jury in October, only to be told the next day that my appearance had been cancelled--much to my relief.

After Nancy Luque sent the letter requesting that I testify before the Senate committee, I once again turned to my trusted friend, Dale Minami, to help me prepare to testify and make a strong statement before the committee. Dale told me he was stunned by my demeanor during the start of our practice session in his office. He described me as timid, acquiescent, and compliant. My voice was shaky and tiny and I was so nervous that I was not thinking about the question being asked, but simply agreeing to everything out of fear. He accurately analyzed that I had developed a great agreeable personality, almost to a fault, derived from my childhood, and while this behavior helped me to succeed, it could be deadly in front of a hostile committee. He was so on target in seeing through my fear and weakness, I completely broke down in tears in front of him. But I was able to regain my composure, knowing this was the "kick in the butt" I needed to get myself together again.

Dale spent hours reminding me of my core strength and of the experiences that helped me survive and achieve all my life, and how I should tap into that same core strength to testify from the position of strength and outrage on behalf of the questioning, the racial tinge of the investigation, and the intimidation of honorable citizens. He also instilled in me a sense of responsibility I owed to my own community as possibly being the only public witness who could speak up for the entire community before the Senate committee. By the time our session ended Dale said he saw a transformation in my body language, facial expression, and speech that indicated I started to believe in myself again.

After all this preparation, the Senate committee never interviewed me and never followed through on my request to testify. I had mixed feelings of relief and disappointment.

I also never received a request to be interviewed by the FBI, which was required of many of my APIA colleagues who worked in the Clinton administration. By this time, I believe there were so many other high-profile wealthy APIA targets being investigated and scrutinized by the press, my role was now considered old news and less significant.

However, in November, when the House started its committee hearings, Nancy was notified that the House committee staff wanted to interview me, so I was not in the clear yet. Nancy arranged for my interview to take place at Dale Minami's office, and he would serve as my counsel, saving me the expense of paying for Nancy's hours and flight to California. Dale called me in to coach me on how to conduct myself during the interview.

As we role-played how I was to conduct myself during this interview, Dale taught me valuable lessons about answering questions versus volunteering information. He asked me, "Is this desk before me black?" I said, "No, it is brown." He said, "Wrong answer. I did not ask you what color the desk was; I simply asked you if the desk was black. The correct answer is no."

As it was, the only interview I had was with a House committee investigator in Dale's office in San Francisco. I followed Dale's instructions to a tee in answering the investigator's questions. I did make Dale flinch one time, when I apologized because I could not recall something. I forgot that I should never apologize and just state the answer. However, Dale's lessons paid off, because that interview was the one and only time I was ever questioned about my role in this scandal.

· · ·

During the start of the Senate hearings in July 1997, chaired by former TV actor Sen. Fred Thompson, Senator Daniel Akaka from Hawaii made a courageous and eloquent statement to appeal to the public as well as those involved in the investigations to refrain from making assumptions and forming stereotypes based on racial and ethnic backgrounds and assigning guilt by ethnic association.

However, the monthly onslaught of daily headlines targeting Asian figures caught up in the illegal fundraising in all the major newspapers, combined with cover stories in every major news magazines with sinister Asian faces and conspiracy theories of foreign influence took a toll on the entire Asian American community in the country. The scandal just perpetuated the stereotype that all Asian Americans are foreigners and not Americans.

· · ·

To make matters worse, at the end of 1996, before the hearings started, in an effort to control the allegations of illegal campaign donations, the Democratic National Committee (DNC) launched an audit of several hundred donors with Asian surnames whose backgrounds had not been vetted thoroughly, according to DNC Chairman Don Fowler. However, the Asian Americans who were audited were appalled by the manner they were questioned about their background, social security numbers, and requests to check their credit records. "People felt it was like a police interrogation," quoted Stewart Kwoh of the Asian Pacific American Legal Center.

Some Asian American DNC donors were so angry that they simply asked that their contributions be returned.

Going through my personal ordeal as a member of the executive committee of the Democratic National Committee, combined with my disappointment in the DNC's lack of response to the negative portrayal of the Asian American voters, was enough for me to tender my resignation from the Executive committee.

Steve Grossman was now the chair of the DNC, and I called him to tell him how angry I was over how the DNC had tried to distance itself from my community and, to this date, had not taken responsibility for not carefully vetting contributions from the John Huang events, an action which could have avoided this catastrophe.

I was prepared to call a press conference as a member of the DNC executive committee for eight years, citing my reasons for resigning from this organization in protest. During this time, it was almost unheard of for any executive committee member to voluntarily resign from the most powerful Democratic committee in the U.S.

Grossman, who inherited this problem from the former chair, Don Fowler, was extremely compassionate and apologetic and understood my position. He was committed to issuing a public apology to the Asian American community and asked for suggestions on how to make amends, with the hope that I would change my mind about the press conference.

I suggested that he meet with APIA Democratic leaders around the country to express the apology and prepare a list of deliverables that would make the APIA Democrats feel they are valued by the party. I told him the most profound way the DNC can show its sincerity is to reinstate the APIA Caucus as an official caucus of the party. He agreed and tried to talk me out of resigning. I told him I am through with national politics, but in return for his commitment, I canceled the press conference and simply submitted my letter of resignation.

On September 25, 1997, Steve Grossman kept his word and the Asian Pacific Islander American Caucus of the Democratic National Committee conducted its first meeting with the adoption of its bylaws at the Omni Shoreham Hotel in Washington DC.

The silence from the White House and the Democratic National Committee in support of the right of all Asian Americans to participate in the political process was deafening. Even more disappointing, the scandal was halting APIA appointments to key positions in the administration.

Hoyt Zia, an appointee, and first president of the National Asian Bar Association, was a lone voice in calling out the administration for their lack of support for the APIA community, a community that had played a major role in the successful election of this administration. Instead of receiving accolades, Hoyt was chastised by some of his fellow APIA appointees within the administration who preferred to not "make waves."

But the escalation of the impact of the negative perception of the Asian American community also exposed the community's weaknesses and inability to quickly counter punch to neutralize attacks on the community's image. Some renowned APIA commentators such as Frank Wu, William Wong, Emil Guillermo, Stewart Kwoh, Dale Minami and Phil Nash wrote eloquent pieces on the subject, but most of their articles were only carried by ethnic press.

There was no institution serving as the national voice of the APIA community. This crisis forced the community to do some deep soul searching, causing some of the community's leaders to wonder if there were a lack of moral courage and leadership in the APIA community.

Finally, in an unprecedented action, on September 11, 1997, a broad coalition of Asian Pacific Islander American (APIA) leaders and national APIA organizations announced the filing of a civil rights complaint with the U.S. Commission on Civil Rights, an independent bipartisan agency that monitors the enforcement of federal civil rights laws with the power to hold public investigative hearings. Simultaneous press conferences announcing the civil rights petition took place in Washington D.C., Los Angeles, Chicago, Boston, and in New York City with Rev. Jesse Jackson.

Helen Zia, famed author of bestsellers, "Asian American Dreams" and "The Last Boat out of Shanghai," coordinated all the media and logistics pertaining to the official filing of this civil rights complaint.

The 27-page petition was authored by two of the most respected APIA civil rights attorneys in the country, Ed Chen, with the American Civil Liberties Union, and Dale Minami, with the law firm of Minami, Lew, and Tamaki of San Francisco.

The petition argued that the APIA community had been unfairly targeted and distressed by a harmful racial climate, citing the following examples:

• Legislative proposals in Congress treating all legal permanent residents as presumptive foreign agents, which is a violation of the First Amendment, according to the petition.

• Congressional hearings on campaign finance with an unfair focus on Asian Pacific Americans, whereas a number of questionable foreign interest contributions from non-Asian sources were ignored such as Thomas Kramer, a German national, who was fined the largest ever penalty for violations of laws against foreign contributions, and yet no testimony was taken in this case with no plans to investigate German Americans. Sen. Bob Dole's campaign fundraiser Simon Fireman was fined a record $6 million for wrongful donations but received no mention during the hearing.

• Racial remarks by politicians and candidates and the news media perpetuating stereotypes, including a national magazine cover with caricature figures of Bill and Hillary Clinton wearing coolie hats with faces of exaggerated Asian features and Asian clothing.

• News reports that linked Asian Pacific Americans alleged to have committed improprieties with other Asian Pacific Americans primarily because of their shared racial background rather than by any significant connection, which resulted in an increased treatment of Asian Pacific Americans as suspected criminals simply because of their race or association with individuals who are alleged to have committed misconduct. A clear example of this anti-Asian sentiment was when Yvonne Lee, a member of the U.S. Civil Rights Commission with a security clearance to enter the White House, was stopped at the entrance because the security guard changed her status to "foreign visitor" based on her Asian surname.

The petition concluded that the combined impact of these numerous acts had a restrictive effect on APA political involvement and the exercise of their rights, as guaranteed by the Constitution.

At the Oct. 10th meeting of the U.S. Commission on Civil Rights, the commission accepted the petition and warned Congress, the major political parties, public officials, and the news media that they must act responsibly and cautiously in their discussion and debates involving Asian Pacific Americans. The commission was particularly concerned that such intolerance and bigotry could have a chilling effect on APA political participation.

. . .

The Commission agreed to hold a briefing in December on alleged incidents cited in the petition, a major victory for the newly formed national coalition of APIA organizations and leaders. On

December 9, the APIA civil rights organizations had a chance to have their say before a national public forum.

The APIA community was well represented by Michael Woo, the first Asian American elected to the Los Angeles City Council; Dr. Ling Chi Wang, head of Asian American Studies at UC Berkeley; Frank Wu, associate law professor at Howard University; Helen Zia, Bay Area freelance writer and contributing editor to *Ms.* magazine; William Woo, *San Francisco Examiner* columnist; Joann Lee, director of journalism at Queen's College; and Daphne Kwok, executive director of the Organization of Chinese Americans.

But, perhaps the most poignant statement came from journalist and author Helen Zia, who cited during her testimony at the hearing, "Most disturbing to me about the media fairness issue is this: the lack of voice given to the Asian American viewpoint to the public by the very institutions entrusted to protect free speech."

Surely, this public protest that attracted national media attention was a wake-up call that the Asian Pacific American community, once called the silent model minority, was finally finding its voice and would fight for its civil rights like never before. As a result, Congress and the media became more conscientious to racial tone for the remainder of the investigative hearing.

AFTERMATH

After months of Senate governmental committee hearings, which generated significant media and public exposure regarding the Asian connection to illegal campaign contributions to the Democratic National Committee, the Senate committee issued its final report in February of 1998.

It concluded that it could not establish that the Chinese government, "...funded, directed, or encouraged the illegal contributions." According to the *New York Times*, "Although the report draws many connections between Chinese interests and various Democratic donors and fund-raisers, it fails to provide evidence that China's government succeeded in funneling money into national campaigns or in influencing policy decisions in Washington."

The article went on to say that the committee never addressed the motives of all the main players in the campaign finance case and was unable to cite instances in which the targeted illegal donors tried to influence government policy toward China or any other country.

The House Committee on Oversight's hearings on campaign finance reform did not fare any better and eventually closed down, after bitter partisan bickering with finger-pointing among the

Democrats and Republicans as to which party was more guilty in using foreign donors and abusing "soft money."

There was some limited success with both committees' investigations, which addressed the systemic breakdown of the country's campaign finance laws and found that both parties engaged in violations with other foreign countries. But the focus on the Asian American community made it a convenient political scapegoat, which helped turn a blind eye to the many campaign finance abuses which did not involve Asian sources.

The only individual I see from time to time now is John Huang and his wife Jane, who travel back and forth between the U.S. and China, where John has a consulting business. His once prestigious and respected life in the U.S. changed forever because of the notoriety of the campaign finance investigation. But when I see him, he never complains and holds no resentment toward the White House or the political institutions that deserted him. If anything, John continues to feel guilty that his actions created such a stigma to the community he so loved.

There are still mixed feelings in the APIA community about John's actions. However, he has a base of supporters who remember him as a proud Asian American who pursued political empowerment for his community. In an eloquent *Asian Week* editorial piece written by Hoyt Zia, Hoyt states in John's defense that, despite his transgressions, "John believed in the importance of political empowerment for the community and recognized the dominant role that money played in obtaining it. He devoted himself to raising the campaign contributions that would get Asian Pacific Islander Americans a seat at the national political table and make the Asian community more than a bystander in national politics."

Los Angeles Times reporters Connie Kang, David Rosenzweig, and Alan Miller wrote the most insightful and thoughtful article about John Huang's history, personality, drive, and motives in an August 3, 1997, article, which helped restore some of my faith in mainstream's media's fairness in reporting.

Their article concludes with the following quote John Huang used before addressing an Asian American community event during the time he was the DNC vice chair of finance:

"America is our country. This is the country that has given us the economic opportunities and political freedom which we could not find elsewhere in the world. We all want to reciprocate to this land. (At) the same time, no one should deprive us of the privilege to participate in the process."

To this day I believe that John Huang, Maria Hsia, James Riady, and the Pacific Leadership Fund donors believed there needed to be a financial investment in helping the APIA community educate their community about the value of political participation, develop leadership, and form an organizational structure to realize their electoral potential. Unfortunately, their methodology to raise political contributions reflected an ignorance of U.S. campaign finance laws, and they neglected to understand the differences between the culture in Asia and the Western culture as it relates to governance and transparency in politics.

...

This personal episode proved to be one of the most devastating experiences in my life, one that even surpassed the turbulence I endured during my childhood and youth. To have one's reputation questioned and maligned in such a high-profile public manner involving the highest court of public opinion in the country was terrifying. And yet, this experience helped me learn how to conquer and overcome fear which has made me that much stronger as a human being. I read that, "You have to have faith that there is a reason you go through certain things. I can't say I'm glad to go through pain, but, in a way one must, in order to gain courage and really feel joy." This experience will also be a constant reminder of how much a touch of human kindness during time of adversity can make the difference between survival and despair. I am so fortunate.

BOOK FIVE

Memorable reflections…

"Some memories are unforgettable, remaining ever vivid and heartwarming."
—Joseph B. Wirthen

STATE PERSONNEL BOARD

"The value of a promise is the cost to you of keeping your word"
—Brian Tracy

In 2003, Dean Lan and Elaine Chiao, co-founders of the Asian Pacific State Employees Association, invited me to lunch to discuss a vacancy on the State Personnel Board (SPB). They had just met with the Governor Gray Davis' appointment secretary, Mike Yamaki, to discuss the possibility of the governor appointing the first APIA to the five-member board which over sees the California state civil service merit system. In spite of APIA representing over 14% of the state civil service employees, no APIA had ever served on this board in its 65-year history.

Michael Yamaki and I had met when Georgette and I put together the first statewide APIA Democratic Conference in 1982. Yamaki made a name for himself in state politics by raising a substantial amount of dollars for Jerry Brown's first run for governor. When Brown was elected, Yamaki, a well-known Los Angeles attorney, played a major role in helping expand the number of APIA judicial appointments representing Southern California, while the Asian Bar Association of the Greater Bay Area worked with Governor Jerry Brown to appoint historic APIA judicial appointments in Northern

California. This joint effort helped Governor Jerry Brown transform the ethnic landscape of California's judicial branch. Eventually the Asian Bar Association of the Greater Bay Area became the start of the National Asian Pacific Bar Association.

I was a friend of Gray Davis from his Assembly days and I had helped with his gubernatorial campaign so Yamaki advised Dean and Elaine that I would be their best chance to get an Asian American on the board.

When I was approached by Dean and Elaine, I told them I was not interested in an appointment as I had just retired to help raise my grandson but, told them I would urge Yamaki to find an Asian American candidate for this seat. When I spoke to him about this issue, Yamaki, in his inimitable blunt fashion, told me that if it was so important to have an Asian American on the board then I needed to put my money where my mouth was and put my hat in the ring for the position because I would have the best chance of being appointed by Governor Davis.

When Yamaki told Governor Davis that I might be interested in the State Personnel Board appointment, the Governor advised Yamaki that he preferred me to serve on the more prestigious Public Utilities Commission. The Governor was having some problems with the existing board and wanted someone who had a strong administrative and political background that he could trust to fill the vacancy.

I told Yamaki I was not interested in the PUC appointment because it was a full-time position based in the Bay Area. Yamaki cautioned me that my turning down the PUC appointment may hurt my chances for the SPB appointment. When I still refused, Lynn Schenck, Governor Davis' chief of staff, called to personally persuade me to take the PUC position. I told Lynn that I simply did not have the qualifications and expertise to serve on the Public Utilities Commission because I barely knew how to "screw in a lightbulb." Lynn was so shocked at my frank response that she broke out laughing and said it was refreshing to hear someone acknowledge a lack of expertise for such an influential appointment.

Subsequently, I was offered the SPB appointment, thanks to the additional persuasion of Davis' campaign manager, Garry South. Even though I was initially reluctant to take this appointment, I felt I had a duty to my community to serve and felt very honored and privileged to become the first Asian American to serve on this board.

When I joined SPB, Bill Elkins, a close ally to the late Mayor Tom Bradley, was the chair. Sean Harrigan, an executive with United Food and Commercial Workers, and Ron Alvarado, a former deputy secretary of Health and Welfare under Gov. Wilson, occupied two additional seats, and I filled out the 4th seat, with one vacancy remaining. The SPB has a seat on the powerful CalPERS (California Public Employees Retirement System) board of trustees, the largest pension fund in the nation. Sean Harrigan was serving as the SPB representative and was subsequently elected the chair of CalPERS.

At the end of 2003, right before the elections of new officers for SPB, Harrigan asked me, Elkins, and Alvarado if we would support him for one last year on the CalPERS board. Elkins and Alvarado did not object so I did not see why I should object in light of his already having three votes to prevail. At that time, there was still a vacancy on the State Personnel Board because of the sudden recall election that Davis lost to Arnold Schwarzenegger. Alvarado told me that the new governor would be appointing Republican Anne Sheehan to fill the fifth spot on the board just in time for the election of officers in December.

We were in San Francisco for our December SPB meeting and the board was enjoying its traditional Christmas dinner together when my husband Ron called to tell me that Willie Brown was trying to reach me at home. It was late in the evening when I returned to the hotel, so I decided to call Willie Brown the next day.

The next morning, I called Willie Brown during our SPB meeting break. Willie Brown explained that he wanted me or Ron Alvarado or the governor's new appointee, Anne Sheehan, to take over as the representative to CalPERS in place of Sean Harrigan. Ron, Anne, and I would have the three votes to oust Harrigan. I believe the purpose of this move was to allow CalPERS to elect another president to replace Harrigan and that choice could possibly be Willie Brown himself, a member of the board at that time. I explained to him, no one had ever approached me about this plan and we just completed our election of officers as the first order of business that morning, so it was too late. Ron Alvarado and Bill Elkins were already committed to supporting Harrigan so the point was moot.

I felt completely blindsided when Willie Brown suddenly flew into a tirade at me over the phone as if I betrayed him. I was speechless and dumbfounded. I simply said I was sorry but, what was done was done.

When Willie Brown found out that I was the person who actually nominated Harrigan's reappointment to the CalPERS board, before he had talked to me, Willie Brown became even more furious with me and did not hesitate to let our mutual friends, including my former boss Lou Papan, know how angry he was with me.

Instead of feeling apologetic or intimidated by Willie Brown's wrath, I became incensed that Willie Brown did not respect me enough to discuss this request with me in advance. Instead, he assumed he could call me the night before the vote and I would instantly acquiesce to his command as if I were still a staffer.

I wrote Willie Brown a letter to let him know exactly how I felt about this last-minute request and, in no uncertain terms, made clear I did not deserve his tongue lashing or anger. I had already committed to Sean Harrigan that I would support him for one more year before I was ever aware of Willie's last-minute scheme to get Harrigan off CalPERS. I made sure Willie Brown knew that even if he had reached me the evening before the vote, it would not have changed my position because I gave Harrigan my word. Ironically it was Willie Brown who taught me, "In politics, your word is your word."

I copied my letter to Willie Brown to Lou Papan who knew that I was quite able to hold my own with legislators, but my weakness had been standing up to Willie Brown. Papan called to tell me he was proud that I was able to finally hold my own with Willie Brown and he was sure Willie would get over his anger. Unfortunately, Willie Brown never responded to my letter and we did not speak for over three years. As years passed, we made amends, but I never felt that our relationship was the same.

...

The next year as we were discussing the election of State Personnel Board officers, Ron Alvarado, a Republican appointee, told me that when Gov. Davis was elected, Ron was the CalPERS board representative until Gov. Davis asked him to step down mid-term to allow Davis' new appointee, Sean Harrigan, to serve on the CalPERS board instead. Alvarado was under no legal obligation to step down, as the State Personnel Board is an independent quasi-judicial board, but he stepped down in deference to Davis' request.

At the end of 2004, Ron Alvarado only had one more year on SPB. He indicated he would like to serve on the CalPERS board another year before his SPB term expired since Sean Hannigan indicated to us this would be his last year.

After my conversation with Ron Alvarado, Sean Harrigan unexpectedly asked me if I would support him for a sixth year. I told him Ron Alvarado had already asked for my support because it was our understanding that this was going to be Harrigan's last year on the CalPERS board. Harrigan already solicited President Bill Elkins' support without Ron's or my knowledge. However, I knew Anne Sheehan would support Ron Alvarado because of their political affiliation and personal relationship, which left me to be the deciding vote.

Harrigan was a forceful but controversial figure on the CalPERS board, but was heavily supported by labor and Democrats. He was aware of my strong Democratic ties and decided to use this as leverage to convince me to change my position.

During my vacation in Hawaii and over the Thanksgiving holidays I began to get calls from a multitude of friends serving in the U.S. Senate, Congress and state legislature, including powerful labor leaders and Democratic Party leaders.

Friends like Norm Mineta, Gary Locke, Congressman Mike Thompson, Speaker Nancy Pelosi, U.S. Sen. Barbara Boxer, State Senators John Burton, Don Perata, and my mentor Art Torres, all called to plead with me to change my position. However, when I explained my position on this issue with regards to fairness and honoring my word, most of my friends who called understood and did not chastise me for standing my ground.

...

As the largest pension fund in the nation, the CalPERS made headline news in the print media and financial journals over the potential ousting of its powerful president. I was named as the deciding vote who could change the leadership of CalPERS. Rumors and innuendoes as to the motive behind my pending vote were swirling out of control. The rumors included:

1) a conspiracy with Governor Schwarzenegger to get rid of Harrigan; 2) the Walt Disney corporation was behind my vote to get rid of Harrigan; 3) I cut a deal with the two Republicans on the board to serve as the next CalPERS representative even though my seniority would make me the next in line; and 4) I was negotiating a gubernatorial appointment for my husband.

I can imagine how ironical this situation must have been to Willie Brown who had attempted to persuade me to take this action the year before.

One learns in politics that the best way to address innuendoes and rumors is to face them head on with the press when legally possible. Therefore, before I cast my vote, I made a press statement to clarify why I was going to support Alvarado versus Harrigan. Harrigan and others continued to spin the theory that this was a conspiracy orchestrated by Governor Schwarzenegger. Some media sources continued to speculate about why a party loyalist would take such a controversial position, incurring the wrath of labor and her own political party.

Whether my position was politically correct or incorrect was less important to me than the fairness issue. I felt my first obligation was to protect the integrity of the State Personnel Board's process of insuring that each SPB member had a fair and equal opportunity to represent SPB on the CalPERS board. Even though I went through a lot of agony and political chastising over this one vote, I have no regrets.

I had made headlines before and did not enjoy it. No one likes to see one's name in the media on controversial issues, especially Asian Americans who are taught not to be the "nail that stands out on a piece of wood." But I also learned in high stakes politics, one cannot be governed by whether or not a decision will cause attention or be ignored. It is more important to make a decision in terms of one's conscience of what is right.

My term with the State Personnel Board ended in 2018 and, as I look back, it was a most rewarding experience working with a board of committed and dedicated colleagues such as the late Bill Elkins, Ron Alvarado, Sean Harrigan, Anne Sheehan, Pat Clarey, Richard Costigan, Kimiko Burton, and Laurie Shanahan. When I started with the board it was an archaic 65-year-old, poorly managed organization that invited cronyism among its long-term staff. Under the leadership of the current management team and my fellow board members, there has been success in reshaping the image of SPB. And with the help of current day technology they have brought the organization up to the standards of the 21st century. It has been an honor and a privilege to have served on this board that protects the merit principles governing over 250,000 state civil service employees.

CalPERS
(California Public Employees Retirement System)

"Your work is going to fill a large part of your life, and the only way to be truly satisfied is to do what you believe is great work." — Steve Jobs

The California Public Employees' Retirement System (CalPERS) serves more than 1.9 million members in its retirement system and administers health benefits for more than 1.4 million members and their families, making it the largest defined-benefit public pension system in the United States.

There are 13 members of the CalPERS board. Six members are elected by all or part of active and retired employees, two are appointed by the governor, one is appointed by the Legislature, two are office holders (treasurer and controller), and two are representatives from human resources and the State Personnel Board.

In 2006, it was my turn to represent the State Personnel Board on the CalPERS Board of Trustees. I was not looking forward to serving on this board after my two years of personal trauma endured over the State Personnel Board's representation on CalPERS. I also knew I had a steep learning curve in entering this new world of finance and investment. It required me to assume fiduciary responsibility overseeing one of the largest pension funds in the world.

My husband always handled all the family finances and investments. I had no real exposure to this world and was anxious about my lack of knowledge, and even more concerned that my peers on the board would see how ignorant I was. My friend, Ginger Lew, was most excited about my joining the CalPERS board. As you'll recall, we had forged a close friendship after she introduced me to national politics in the 80s. She was the highest-ranking APIA woman appointee of a cabinet agency during the Clinton administration. After she left her position in the administration, she joined the private sector as the CEO and then partner of two venture capital funds. Her success in this field gained her recognition as one of the few Asian American woman fund managers during this era.

Through our conversations, Ginger sensed my feeling of inadequacy in this new role. As the former co-chair of the NASDAQ Listing Council and the former chair of a European based investment fund, she knew exactly what types of fiduciary issues I would be facing on this board. To help me, she flew out from Washington prior to my starting on CalPERS and provided me with a PowerPoint presentation about CalPERS and its entire investment structure. To this day I still have her presentation.

I also faced the challenge of understanding the intricacies of the health care delivery systems because CalPERS was responsible for the management of health benefits for all California public employees, retirees, and families. Thankfully, I had my in-home-expert husband, Ron, who at this time was one of the most knowledgeable health care lobbyists in the Capitol.

...

When I attended my first board meeting, I could sense that I carried a bit of notoriety as the person who ousted former board president Sean Harrigan. The board was heavily influenced by long time senior members of the board who had over a decade of service, such as the late Bob Carlson, George Diehr, the late Charles Valdes, and Kurato Shimada. The state treasurer's and state controller's representatives carried a different level of influence because they represented their bosses' agendas on the board.

The other board members, some elected and some appointed, were relative newcomers to the board and were considered the new guard when I joined. Rob Feckner, who was an officer of the California Schools Employees Association, succeeded Harrigan as the new president of the board. He immediately made me feel welcome.

As president, Feckner had the daunting task of trying to bridge the gap between the old guard, the new guard, and the elected state constitutional officers on the board.

I confessed to Feckner that I had much to learn about CalPERS, to the point that when I heard the word "hedge," as in hedge fund, I was thinking about a "bush." Feckner immediately registered me in the Fiduciary College program at Stanford Law School to help me gain a better understanding of my new role. I attended this intensive program with another new trustee, Tony Oliviera, a King's County supervisor from Fresno who was an appointee of Governor Arnold Schwarzenegger. As a result of taking this program together, Tony—a successful rancher and businessman with a major in economics—became my closest ally and adviser on the board

As I continued to educate myself on the inner workings of CalPERS, trying to learn as much as I could about every aspect of finance, investment, and health care, I saw myself emerge as an independent member under no pressure from any special interest groups which allowed me to simply take positions on issues that I felt best served the state employees I represented on the board.

President Rob Feckner recognized my passion regarding diversity and appointed me as the diversity advisor to the board.

This allowed me to carve a role for myself as a spokesperson for CalPERS on its leadership on diversity to special interest groups and public forums.

After completing my 2-year term on CalPERS board, I was asked by state Controller John Chiang to serve as one of his advisors on CalPERS issues, so I continued my participation on the board as a representative of John Chiang, along with Terry McGuire, the deputy state controller representative on the board.

John Chiang has always been a champion in promoting the value of diversity and inclusion. I encouraged John, who served on both the CalPERS and CalSTRS boards, to sponsor initiatives with CalPERS and CalSTRS to promote and encourage corporate board diversity. Through John's leadership, both boards adopted resolutions advancing these goals through their investment channels with Fortune 500 companies.

...

When I joined CalPERS in 2006, it was known to have one of the most diverse pools of investment managers in the U.S. I learned that during recent years, large pension funds, endowments, foundations, and institutional investors such as CalPERS have embarked on outreach programs to increase their access to qualified, ethnic minority fund managers to better gain access to a broader range of fund managers--those with access to different deal flows. There was also a push for plan sponsors to have qualified fund managers that reflected the demographics of their constituents.

Beginning in the late 1990s, CalPERS was at the forefront of this effort, along with New York, Texas, and other state pension funds which represented heavily diverse populations.

During my very first board meeting, I was planning to simply listen and learn. Senior Investment Officer Leon Shahinian was giving a report on CalPERS' California Initiative Funds, funds earmarked for investments in California-oriented businesses that were currently underrepresented in the Fund's private equity portfolio. Investments were to target small businesses, emerging or developing companies, and other investments with a focus on underserved urban and rural California communities.

The report highlighted how much investment was going to ethnic emerging manager funds for underserved communities that were predominantly Latino and African American, as well as rural communities. But there was no mention of any investment going to any APIA emerging manager funds or underserved communities.

My first public question as a CalPERS board member was asking Leon why there was an absence of APIA investment firms participating in this initiative. Leon carefully explained that it takes a lot of effort to outreach, recruit, and evaluate proposals that provide the right mix of demographics and the right investment management teams. The New American Alliance (NAA), which represented Latino investment firms, and the National Alliance of Investment Companies (NAIC), which represented predominantly African American investment managers, were sources CalPERS utilized to identify and recruit emerging domestic fund managers to bid on RFP's to manage CalPERS funds. CalPERS and other institutional investors worked with these professional organizations to help build a pipeline to reach out to a more diverse pool of fund managers.

I recalled Ginger Lew telling me during her PowerPoint presentation to be aware that Asian Pacific American investment managers were being left out of the loop in terms of investment opportunities because they had no vehicle to help them network, form professional relationships, and learn about new investment opportunities with institutional investors.

So, when I relayed this incident to Ginger, she and I instinctively said to one another, "We need to start an Asian Pacific American investment management organization so institutional investors will no longer have an excuse for the absence of partnerships with Asian American investment teams."

Ginger and I asked the California Asian Pacific Legislative Caucus, led then by Chairman Assemblyman Alberto Torrico, to partner with CalPERS and CalSTRS to sponsor a workshop for Asian Pacific American fund managers to learn how to do business with the two largest pension funds in the nation. Both CalPERS and CalSTRS enthusiastically supported this idea, even providing in-kind support for the event at the CalPERS facility. We had no idea how many people would show up.

The workshop took place in November 2006, and—to our astonishment--drew over 150 APIA fund managers from all over the country. The attendees at this workshop gave CalPERS and CalSTRS the first APIA data base of APIA investment managers to use as a resource, and it gave Ginger and me the impetus to start an organization.

Ginger and I realized that we needed a young team of experienced investment managers to help lead the organization because this was a relatively new profession for APIA, and the median age of APIA investment managers was between the mid-30's to mid-40's. Clayton Jue, the CIO and CEO of Leading-Edge Investment Advisors, was one of the few well-established APIA fund managers in this field. This was probably why he was the only Asian American presenter being featured at the CalPERS diversity conference Ginger and I attended in San Jose.

Clayton, a very studious, soft spoken but eloquent and knowledgeable speaker, impressed both Ginger and me enough to cause us to dash up to the stage at the end of his presentation and basically say, "We would like to talk to you about an idea of starting an organization for Asian American investment managers." Much to Clayton's credit, he agreed to sit down with these two strange women he never met before and quietly listen to our pitch about the need for an Asian American investment manager organization. He was the first person we pitched to help us, so we had no answers to his questions about funding or structure.

But after our discussion, he was all in.

With Clayton's help, we were able to identify three other energetic young APIA investment fund managers in their mid-30s to help us kick start the organization: Brenda Chia, who was then former general partner with Asymmetry Capital partners; Bennett Kim, a young, energetic partner with Big Rock partners; and Gordon Liao, who made a name for himself by authoring a piece on why APIA have a difficult time breaking the glass ceiling. Gordon, who was vice president with Reliant Equity Investors and a former Toigo Fellow, was the perfect fit to help with this effort. To this day, these talented founding board members continue to devote their time and commitment to the growth of the organization.

Ginger and I co-chaired the board at the beginning and Clayton served as president. Clayton generously provided clerical support and office space for the organization. To establish instant credibility for the organization to attract members, we developed an honorary board led by former Transportation Secretary Norman Y. Mineta. Board members included Ambassador Linda Tsao Yang, former head of the Asian Development Bank and chair of the Asian Corporate Governance Association; Dr. Ta-Lin Hsu, CEO of H&Q Asia Pacific; Guy Kawasaki, managing director of Garage Technology Ventures; and Steve Westly, founder and CEO of the Westly Group.

Today, Mineta, Tsao Yang, and Ta-Lin Hsu still serve as honorary board members.

The six founding board members named the organization the Association of Asian American Investment Managers (AAAIM) with a goal of elevating and increasing the visibility of APIA fund professionals to institutional investment funds. The organization wanted to serve as a conduit, fostering education, collaboration, and partnership between large sources of capital and the talent, experience, and skills of Asian American investment professionals.

In 2007, after a year of organizing, AAAIM launched two networking opportunities for APIA fund managers and LP's, one at the Harvard Club in New York and one at the Ritz Carlton hotel in San Francisco. Attendance started slowly, with just 50-75 participants during the first two events, and fundraising was difficult, but this board of young enthusiastic professionals was not deterred.

Brenda Chia took on two roles to help the organization grow. She served as president and was primarily responsible for organizing the conferences, outreach, and fundraising; as well as serving on the board. Her leadership during this time was invaluable and critical to AAAIM's successful launch. As the organization grew, AAAIM was able to hire a full-time president to handle its day- to-day operation.

Twelve years later, AAAIM has grown from 150 subscribers to 3,000. Each conference has been sold out, requiring larger venues each year. Additionally, under Gordon Liao's leadership, AAAIM added the Emerging Leadership Initiative to its program to provide leadership skills to young and midlevel professionals to help position them in executive and decision-making roles within all realms of the investment management and alternative asset industries. It is considered one of the most successful components of AAAIM.

AAAIM is now recognized by the finance/investment industry and national financial institutions as the voice of Asian American investment managers.

...

I had awakened to a whole new world of finance and investment during my brief time with CalPERS. This experience gave me an opportunity to work with Ginger Lew in building an organization for APIA professionals to have a representative voice within the financial and investment institutions of this country. Serving on the CalPERS board proved to me that professional growth does not stop after retirement. Instead, retirement gives one a choice of expanding one's horizons and seizing every opportunity to continue to make a difference and help make a positive impact on someone, somewhere, somehow.

AAAIM board of directors, Sanjiv K. Shah, Bennett Kim, Gordon Liao, me, Ginger Lew, and Clayton Jue

FIRST TRIP TO CHINA

San Francisco Supervisor Tom Hsieh was one of the first Asian Americans to recognize the importance of creating more Asian American visibility within the Democratic National Committee to counter the proliferation of Asian Americans being recruited into the Republican National Committee during the 1980s.

Tom, who took great interest in my dedication to empower APIA in state politics, nominated me to join a delegation of the American Council of Young Political Leaders (ACYPL) on a visit to China in 1982. This prestigious program, based in Washington D.C., focuses on international educational exchanges for young political leaders worldwide who have the potential to become tomorrow's global leaders and policy makers.

I didn't envision myself as a potential global leader and was wondering if I would be out of place with the members of the delegation who were either elected officials or high-ranking executives from Washington. This also was my first exposure to the inside-the-beltway political environment.

The delegation was bipartisan, with the leader of the group coming from the party of the sitting president. In this case, under President Ronald Reagan, the U.S. treasurer, Angela "Bay" Buchanan (sister to noted Republican political pundit Patrick

Buchanan) was selected to lead. The rest of the delegation was evenly split between Democrats and Republicans. The Democratic members were Lanny Davis, who eventually became chief counsel to President Clinton and now to the infamous Michael Cohen; Alan Karcher, speaker of the House in New Jersey; Jim Rosapepe, an attorney who presently serves as a state senator in Maryland and was the former ambassador to Romania; Deborah McCune, a state representative of Arizona; and Jim Martin, a state representative of New Mexico.

The Republicans were Margaret Tutwiler, chief of staff to Jim Baker; Justin Wilson, a prominent attorney and business man from Nashville, Tennessee, who now serves as state comptroller of Tennessee; Randal Teague, former chief of staff to Congressman Jack Kemp; and Jim Barnes, who was then chief counsel to the U.S. Dept. of Agriculture.

Our host in China was the All China Youth Federation and our escorts were staff of China's foreign ministry.

Since this trip took place in 1982, when China was just beginning to open up its gates to the outside world, our delegation was led by a White House official so that we would be treated as state officials hosted by the U.S. ambassador, allowing us the opportunity to meet with China's leading party leaders. The experience of being in this Communist country, during a period when China was still a mystery to the majority of the outside world, made us aware of how tightly controlled our itinerary was--who we visited and what we saw regarding education, housing, manufacturing, and governmental programs. We were given little time to wander and tour on our own, and we felt that we were being very closely monitored, even within the privacy of our hotel rooms.

We were especially sensitive to the third world living conditions of the masses and the tremendous need for modernizing this country's infrastructure, to the point that a facility's having an American toilet was a sign of luxury on the trip.

With the sight of thousands of bicycles as China's primary form of transportation for the common people, and the old, dilapidated buildings everywhere, it was as if we were stepping back in time. Crowds would surround us everywhere, curious about the way we dressed and behaved. One of the most memorable moments of the trip was our climb up the Great Wall which reminded us of the perseverance and the amazing use of human resources of this country to build a wall that can be seen from space.

I could tell by the reactions of the Chinese officials and people on the street that I was identified as an American first who happens to be Chinese. Ironically, in the U.S., I am seen as a Chinese foreigner first and not as an American.

Our Chinese guides from the foreign ministry were curious about my life as a Chinese American in a country where we were a minority group. As the trip progressed, our two main guides and I discussed the differences in lifestyle for Chinese citizens versus Chinese Americans in the U.S. One of our guides, Xia Jihue, later came to visit my family in Sacramento when she was granted an official exchange to study here in the U.S.

I was very surprised and touched that, through the State Department's vetting of my background, our China hosts were informed of my father's identity. One host arranged for me to have a private lunch with China's most famous Cantonese Opera diva, Hung Seen Nuey, who was treated like a heroine because of her early defection to Communist China from Hong Kong before they sealed the border. At the luncheon, she told me of my father's fame and tragic passing and gave me one of his recordings.

There was no hint of apology for the circumstances of his death—which made this a touching but awkward encounter for me.

Being the only Chinese American among this prestigious group of fellow delegates gave me some stature because they relied on me to coach them regarding proper Chinese social protocol when meeting our official hosts. Even more important, I was able to describe some of the mysterious food items we were being served at each elaborate ten course banquet hosted every evening and provide them messages to use for the toast as each entrée was served.

Treasurer Bay Buchanan was pregnant with her first child during the trip and asked me to sit next to her at all the formal meals because she wanted me to taste each food course before she ate hers. I made sure each host knew of her condition and explained she would be unable to eat strange delicacies such as webbing between ducks' feet, bird's nest soup, or any snake dish.

All delegates were forewarned that we needed to bring gifts that represented our country to exchange with each city's host committee. Bay had the best gifts, including jars of jellybeans signed by President Reagan and a framed dollar bill with her signature on it. I tried to avoid standing next to Bay when we did our gift exchange to avoid embarrassment, because my gifts were gold bear tie tacks which I passed off as pins: I forgot the men in China wear Mao uniforms, no ties.

...

This experience preceded my entrance into national politics, so it was the very first time I had a chance to personally interact with a group of national political figures. During our down time, socializing with one another, I was hearing personal discussions about the U.S. president, the vice president, and congressional leaders I read about in the papers. And these comments were being made by individuals who interacted with these American politicians daily.

The discussions between the Democrats and Republicans became very heated at times between strong personalities such as Democrats Lanny Davis and Jim Rosapepe and Republicans Bay Buchanan and Margaret Tutwiler. I found myself playing it safe by floating comfortably between both groups, because in my own Asian way, I made sure not to offend anyone with strong political opinions.

During our farewells, I felt that this trip bonded all of us because our opinion of China was forever changed. We gained a deeper respect for China and were able to personally experience the undeniable potential of China to emerge from being an impoverished third world country to becoming a world power.

As Bay and I said goodbye at the airport, she told me that she wanted to find a way for us to stay in touch as we had developed such a close bond during this trip. I felt that these were the usual parting words among individuals who traveled together for three weeks. I never fathomed that in this case, Bay was talking about a presidential appointment for me.

United States Treasurer Angela Bay Buchanan in China

REAGAN

A month after the China trip, my secretary, Grace Yee, told me that someone from the White House was on the phone asking to speak to me. I was thinking maybe it was my friend Ed Rollins, the former director of the Assembly Republican Caucus who was wooed away by the White House when Reagan was elected.

However, the person calling was from presidential personnel, and she was requesting that I submit my papers for consideration for a presidential appointment. I laughed and politely told her that it probably would be a waste of time for her and me because I was a staunch Democrat who was active with the party and worked for a Democratic administration in California under Speaker Willie L. Brown Jr.

She was quite direct, and in her pronounced Southern accent told me that I had already been approved to serve on President Reagan's newly created Advisory Committee on Women's Small Business Ownership, and that I only needed to submit my application form. Now I was really curious, because I did not own a small business and was unable to see the relevance of my professional position at the Capitol bringing value to the subject matter of this committee. However, I told her to send me the application and decided, why not, and sent in my application.

Later in the afternoon, I received a call from Bay Buchanan, and she explained that she was stepping down as U.S. treasurer so she could devote more time to her baby and family. The president wanted to keep her on in some capacity so they created this advisory committee to demonstrate his interest in women's issues, and Bay was to serve as the chair.

Bay confided in me that this commission was going to have some extremely high-powered women entrepreneurs with strong personalities, and she wanted a close ally on the board whom she could trust to serve as her eyes and ears. She thought I would be perfect because of the way I was able to maneuver and remain friends with everyone in the China delegation despite the clashing personalities and partisan bickering.

In November 1983, President Reagan announced my appointment to his Advisory Committee on Women's Business Ownership. It was an interesting group of prominent Republican business supporters of the president, many of whom knew one another as prominent donors to the Republican Party. The only male appointee was Robert McMillan, vice president of public affairs for Avon Products from New York. I immediately bonded with the two other California members, Patricia Nettleship, who was president of her own construction company in Southern California, and Beth Rogers, president of Davis Pacific Corp. in Santa Monica. One of my favorite appointees was Ruth Trotter from Memphis, who was the founder and president of the Stork Shop.

I am sure these women were trying to figure out the rationale behind my appointment. But, seeing how close I was to the chair of the committee, no one questioned my relevancy. However, I gradually found ways to bond with each of the members and found them extremely warm and friendly, even though I was the only Democrat serving on the committee.

The commission's purpose was to conduct hearings around the country to develop a report to the President on issues facing women business owners. But the most exciting experience was getting an invitation to go to the White House to have lunch with the president. This was my first visit to the White House.

I was excited and nervous as we went through security clearance and tried to appear calm as we were ushered into a beautiful waiting room close to the Rose Garden where we were greeted by Craig Fuller, the president's deputy chief of staff.

Coincidentally, I worked with Craig's brother, Bruce Fuller, who was an education consultant in the Assembly, and I used that as an ice breaker when I was introduced to Craig. During Craig's briefing prior to our luncheon with the President, we were told that press would be invited in during our Q&A discussion, and we received strict instructions that if we wanted to ask the president questions during the Q&A period, we needed to write them down in advance and give them to staff before we entered the dining room.

A half-hour later, we were ushered in to await the president. Our name tags with the White House seal were on the table, and I almost sat down until I noticed each person stood behind their chair awaiting the president's entrance.

Once President Reagan arrived, we all took our seats. He started by going around the room asking everyone to introduce themselves. I could tell some women were nervous and the conversation was very formal. When it came to my turn, I told him about my position at the state Capitol, and as soon as I mentioned that I worked for Speaker Willie Brown, his face instantly lit up and he expressed his fondness for working with Willie Brown and included some anecdotes about Willie Brown in the Capitol. I told the president that I must confess I was the only Democrat serving on his committee and I was grateful for the opportunity.

He responded with a big warm smile, "Not to worry," he said, "I was once a Democrat myself." To which I quipped, "What happened to you?" He broke out in raucous laughter, explaining he had finally come to his senses.

As we took pictures with the president, he shook my hand warmly and told me once again how delighted he was that I was serving on the committee and asked me to give his warmest regards to Willie Brown. I left the luncheon totally enamored with someone whose politics were not in sync with mine, but whose charm, personality, and warmth won me over forever as an ardent fan.

After two years of work, this presidential committee produced a report that highlighted economic barriers that faced women in small business. I am grateful that my dear friend, Bay Buchanan, gave me this opportunity to serve on my first presidential committee.

Meeting President Ronald Reagan at the White House

FOURTH UNITED NATIONS WOMEN'S WORLD CONFERENCE

In March of 1995, during the Clinton administration, I was invited to participate in the fourth United Nations World Conference on Women, their final preparatory conference to help create the platform of issues affecting women worldwide, to advance public opinion and policy changes aimed at improving living conditions for women around the world.

The platform would be presented by the United National Fourth World Conference on Women in Beijing for formal adoption by each member nation. I was asked to spend three weeks in New York; delegates stayed at the Helmsley Palace Hotel, which was walking distance to UN Plaza.

The honorary chair of the conference was Hillary Clinton and the administrative conference chair was U.S. Ambassador Madeleine Albright. There was no structured agenda; each delegate was a strong leader in her own right, so it was assumed they knew what to do to get the work done.

I decided to focus on meeting women from the third world Asian countries, since I was the only delegate with Asian ancestry. I was able to exchange ideas with highly educated and influential bi-lingual Asian women who escaped their world of poverty through education, only to return to help their homeland fight to eradicate poverty, famine, and diseases, and advance women's rights. The courage and leadership of these women, many of whom had been abused and whose lives had been threatened for speaking out, forever left an impression and underscored how lucky I was to be an American.

Another highlight of this experience was the chance to interact with Hillary Clinton. We knew each other in passing through the presidential campaign and the numerous White House events I attended, but I never had a chance to talk to her at length. I found her one-on-one persona completely different from her public image. First, she has a great sense of humor. She was like "one of the girls" with our group and personally knew many of the delegates. In our conversations about how I could add value as the only Asian American woman delegate, she was strategic and empathetic at the same time. She was delighted when I told her my daughter wrote an essay describing Hillary as her heroine.

At the time, Hillary was under subpoena to testify in the Whitewater case and, before she left to appear in court, I sent her a personal note of good luck. She responded with a handwritten note and gave her regards to Stephanie. I still have that note on display in my home, along with treasured mementos that reflect the honor I had to work with amazing women leaders around the world and serve as a representative of our country at the United Nations.

Hillary Clinton at the United Nation's Women's World Conference platform meeting in New York

CAMPAIGNS AND ASIAN WEEK

During my era as a legislative staffer, campaigns were considered a part of our life at the Capitol with the understanding that we would use personal time to work on campaigns to help incumbents or candidates endorsed by our immediate bosses or the leadership of the house. Campaign work was grueling, often requiring days away from the family to work in districts, walk precincts, staff the phone bank, put together voter packets, and get out the vote on Election Day. The only breaks we took were for sleep and meals of sandwiches and pizza.

Generally, legislative staffers were relegated to walking the least desirable neighborhood precincts that were too intimidating for the average everyday volunteer. Georgette and I would always volunteer together because we could partner up walking precincts and rooming together. We had our share of frightening moments dropping door hangers reminding people to vote in the wee morning hours, including being mistaken for hookers by truck drivers in a highly questionable district in San Bernardino, even though we were carrying clipboards and holding campaign literature.

However, working campaigns helped me learn the nuts and bolts of running a campaign and proved invaluable as I graduated to advising campaigns targeting the APIA voter bases at the local, state, and national level.

In addition to the Dukakis, Clinton/Gore presidential campaigns, the last two campaigns I worked on were among the most memorable.

The Kevin Johnson Sacramento mayoral campaign was the last campaign Georgette and I worked on together. Despite Kevin Johnson's local celebrity status as an NBA Phoenix Suns all-star basketball player and his philanthropic work revitalizing Oak Park and Sacramento High School, Kevin was somewhat shy and a political novice. But, after he became mayor, he quickly catapulted onto the political stage with great acumen and displayed extraordinary leadership as mayor.

His efforts for Sacramento to retain the Sacramento Kings and build the arena downtown forever changed the economic landscape of downtown Sacramento and further enhanced the economic vibrancy of the city. To this day Georgette and I remain friends with Kevin and his wife, Michelle Rhee. My husband, Ron, continues to serve on the St. Hope Academy board founded by Kevin and managed by his wife, Michelle, who gained national fame as an education reformer in Washington D.C.

I thought the Johnson campaign would be my very last until I received a call from an old colleague who had served as Sen. David Roberti's press secretary, Steve Glazer. After Steve left the Capitol, he became a political consultant, and later was elected to the city council of Orinda, California. A former Brown ally, Steve was tapped by Jerry Brown to run his second gubernatorial campaign. Steve called to ask if I would consider helping the Brown campaign mobilize the APIA voter base, understanding that there was no compensation available for my services. Jerry Brown's campaign was on a tight budget compared to the unlimited funds available to his opponent, Meg Whitman.

The polls were showing that among APIA voters, Brown was only three points ahead of Whitman. I was stunned because I was around the Capitol when Brown's administration made history with his unprecedented number of APIA judicial and executive appointments, including those of Jerry Enomoto as the director of Corrections, Linda Tsao Yang as the Savings and Loans commissioner, and Yori Wada to the U.C. Board of Regents.

The next four months I volunteered full-time, working with campaign staffers Nick Velasquez and John Kim, to remind this generation of APIA voters of Jerry Brown's historic contributions to the APIA community, and helping statewide APIA leaders organize grassroots support for Brown. Bill Wong, political consultant and now political director to California Assembly Speaker Anthony Rendon, worked with the California Democratic Party to strategically target APIA voters. The combined effort resulted in Jerry Brown winning the APIA vote statewide by a margin of 17 points.

Subsequently, Steve Glazer was elected to the state Senate.

...

Campaigns provide unique experiences with so many personalities. But one never forgets the camaraderie and celebrations over victories and the terrible pain and disappointments of defeats. These moments truly represent the heart and soul of politics, which brings me to the late John Fang, founder and publisher of *Asian Week*.

John was one of my heroes when I started in politics in the 70s. He was an early pioneer, championing the need for Asian American involvement in politics and public policy, and he invested private resources to publish the first bi- weekly Chinese/English publication out of a small printing shop on Sacramento Street in San Francisco. John was so proud of my achievements in the state Capitol, he would call me from time to time just to chat about politics. I also became close friends with his sons, James and Ted, who were both active in San Francisco politics and big supporters of my boss, Lou Papan.

In 1987, the Fangs offered me an opportunity to write a monthly political column called "Capitol Watch" to educate their readers on APIA political happenings around the state and country, as well as to reflect my own experiences as a political "insider." The column ran from 1987 to 1995, and then I was asked to resume writing it from 2000 to 2006. I enjoyed the opportunity to share my thoughts about current political issues affecting our community, elected officials and candidates, and electoral politics. I also provided advice about running for office or seeking appointments at the state level. It was flattering to think about the number of people who could be influenced by my column. I had my share of critics who also disagreed with me from time to time; however, as my editor, Samson Wong, would say about my critics, "At least they're reading your column."

BOOK SIX

Living in the present...

"The secret of health for both mind and body is not to mourn for the past, worry about the future, or anticipate troubles, but to live in the present moment wisely."
—Buddha

MENTORSHIP

"Mentoring is a brain to pick, an ear to listen, and a push in the right direction." —John C. Crosby

I have publicly stated many times that the satisfaction I have gained in my career is not based on titles or accomplishments, but more on the pride of seeing how mentorship can help shape the paths of others.

When a person is in a position of influence and power, one can never underestimate how much a moment of attention or advice can mean to a person seeking guidance. I know, because without parental guidance, I totally relied on mentors and role models to help me navigate my own life. Mentoring others to help them realize their potential may have been a way to reinforce my own self esteem.

During one of my hectic chief administrative officer days, my secretary, Grace Yee, asked if I had a moment to say hi to a young woman, the daughter of Connie Pasquil, who worked in the Senate. In bounced this smiling, young, energetic woman who introduced herself in one sentence, and without hesitation added that her mother told her to ask me if I would mentor her. I stopped for moment, but her bright smile, charm, and confident demeanor won me over completely and I could tell there was something special about her.

The rest is history. Today Mona Pasquil is among the most influential Filipina Americans in politics, having served as the former interim lt. governor of California, as well as having served in prominent positions in the White House and the Democratic National Committee. She was Governor Gray Davis' political director and the longest tenured California appointment secretary, serving both Gov. Jerry Brown and Gov. Gavin Newsom. She is among many of the Asian Pacific Legislative Staff Caucus members during this era to emerge as a successful professional political role model within and outside the state Capitol today.

During my public speaking engagements, I am often asked how I, as an Asian American woman, succeeded in breaking the glass ceiling in the state Capitol during a time when women and ethnic minorities were still struggling to find their places. I personally felt the following practices helped me along the way throughout my professional career.

Add value and make a difference.
I believe that luck and timing play a role in a career, but individuals who capitalize on the opportunity to showcase their unique abilities to "add value and make a difference" in the workplace or institution are the most successful. In my case, the absence of APIA influence in the state Capitol during my era gave me the opportunity to help change that void and thus added value to my own professional contribution to the institution.

Know thyself, believe in oneself, and do not let your gender or ethnicity define you.
My strong drive to succeed and achieve derived from my childhood days caused me to constantly evaluate my strengths and weaknesses so I could improve my skills. For example, I had to overcome the

mainstream cultural image of Asian women by working twice as hard to prove that I had the same leadership capabilities as my male counterparts. As a woman, I had to constantly assert myself so that I would be taken seriously. I quickly experienced the double standard related to gender: assertive women would be labeled "bitch," whereas assertive men would be labeled "effective." But I did not allow this mentality to deter me from getting the job done for my bosses and the institution. Eventually, consistency and accomplishments defines one's reputation and credibility.

Surround yourself with people who are smart and complement your skills.

Being able to acknowledge your strengths and weaknesses enables you to seek out staff whose talents and skills complement yours, while at the same time strengthening the capabilities of your team. The smartest people I know are those people who know what they don't know.

Remember the importance of interpersonal skills.

I never saw myself as the "smartest kid on the block"—I was confident of my interpersonal skills because I grew up utilizing my social skills to make friends to fill the void of having no family. I genuinely like people, and how you treat people is generally how people will respond to help you succeed.

As an executive, I always maintained an open-door policy to everyone with no regard to status or rank, especially in the Capitol, where power reigns. I practiced the quote by Maya Angelou, "People will forget what you say and do, but will never forget how you made them feel," which also guided me in my sensitive interactions with the egos of the elected officials I served.

Honesty and integrity are essentials

One of my weaknesses was my need to please people; I was

reluctant to hurt people's feelings or deliver bad news because I always wanted to be liked. But I also had a responsibility to be honest and fair in making administrative decisions. I found it hard to say no. When there were requests that I simply could not justify, I tried to find options that would appease the situation. However, when that did not work, I was the recipient of some angry or retaliatory reactions to my unfavorable decisions.

I had to learn to accept the fact that the higher you ascend on the ladder, the tougher the decisions and the more detractors you will encounter along the way. But ultimately the respect I garnered as a fair and trustworthy administrator justified the means.

Communication skills are a must.
I had no problem with my writing skills. But I had to push myself to learn the art of public speaking and speaking up without being afraid to challenge a higher authority or people who were bolder than I. I learned the importance of expressing myself in a clear, concise manner with a strong voice, direct eye contact, and the right attitude, even though there were times I was shaking inside with fear.

In the beginning, I especially disliked dealing with the press for fear they would misinterpret what I said, or that I would not have the answers to the questions they would pose to me in front of the camera. I also lacked the ability to deliver clever sound bites like so many of my glib predecessors. However, I forced myself to confront this weakness by continuously practicing and learning the skill until it came naturally.

Network, network, network. — Oh, and network.
Networking within and outside the Capitol helped me cultivate a massive support base of people who were helpful whenever I needed their support professionally or personally as an executive. I participated in extracurricular activities such as helping Speaker

Brown produce annual end of the session social events for staff and the public and participating in annual legislative tennis tournaments, all for the sake of networking. Relationships are vital in the Capitol if one wants to succeed.

Prioritize, delegate and trust your team

Learning to prioritize issues, trust your team, and delegate effectively is critical for an executive to succeed. Be clear and consistent with your expectations and provide honest and direct feedback to staff on their job performances.

Equally important is to share the credit for accomplishments with the staff and be willing to protect staff by accepting responsibility for failures, because the "buck stops with you."

Get the job done—and follow through!

I earned a reputation of being a problem solver because, once I focused on an assignment, I left no stone unturned to find a solution. I hated to fail. I quickly learned to "think outside the box" and trust my gut and be creative. However, if for some reason I failed to come through with a timely solution, I was quick to let my superior know so together we would seek outside help for solutions. I also was quick to acknowledge if I made a mistake whether it be with my staff or bosses. These quick admissions often time helped to neutralize the consequences, especially with high-profile, temperamental bosses.

Show loyalty and compassion

Loyalty and compassion are gold, especially in politics, because power and influence can be fleeting and cyclical. I always felt it was my duty to protect the integrity of the institution that I served. And I found that it was equally important to treat all elected members and staff alike, whether they were Democrats or Republicans and whether they were in power or out of power.

In fact, I would pay more attention to individuals who had fallen from grace, because gestures of kindness are most remembered during times of adversity, and this attitude helped me gain a lot of respect within this political institution. I read once, "A word of encouragement during a failure is worth more than an hour of praise after success."

Resiliency, a positive attitude, and a good sense of humor always help.
The late Assemblyman Lou Papan once told me my greatest strength was my resiliency because of how I bounced back from the many challenges and adversities I faced as an Asian American woman executive in the Capitol. But this was the skill I learned growing up. I forced myself not to dwell on the negatives and simply move forward, looking at setbacks as "learning experiences." And what helped me most through the learning experiences was my sense of humor. I used humor often to diffuse a tense or hostile discussion when I felt comfortable the responder would be receptive. Friends also know I laugh at myself a lot because it keeps me sane and grounded and, for me, laughter simply makes life better.

LEADERSHIP AND LESSONS LEARNED

"Leadership is not a position or a title, it is action and example."
—Anonymous

Professionally speaking, in the political arena, leadership is connected to power. For staff positions, power is connected to the level of access and influence one has to those who are the ultimate decision-makers of the institution or organization.

In the Capitol arena of "survival of the fittest," with no civil service protection or job security, your ability to move up depends on your political acumen, a specialized skill or expertise, interpersonal skills, ability to communicate, political networking, and relationships.

When I entered adulthood, I never set out to become a community leader. I was simply interested in succeeding in my professional career in order to become financially stable and enjoy a comfortable normal life with family.

At the community level, my career led me to issues and opportunities where I saw voids that motivated me to want to make changes.

I basically emerged as a leader within the APIA community because I was willing to challenge the status quo. Luckily, I found a partner, Georgette Imura, who shared my passion and vision of change, and together we sought out other champions in the community who knew that our ethnic community was too content to stay silent and not make waves.

Georgette and I were willing to be the 'face" that took the risks, accepted the challenges, and defined the vision so that there was a clear-cut goal to be achieved by the community groups. We listened to our peers, remained open minded to their suggestions, and admitted what we didn't know quickly.

Trust and reliability are important when you want to accomplish something with a group. The first venture into leadership is always the hardest because you have no track record. But once you have accomplished objectives that speak to your leadership, it is easier to find people to help you with your next venture.

And when I define leadership, I believe that, "True leadership is not proving to others how important you are. True leadership is making others feel how important they are to you."

. . .

Looking back, I have asked myself, "What could I have done better?" And the number one answer is that I wish I could have spent more time being a mother to my daughter, Stephanie, during her childhood and youth.

During her most precious years of growing up, I was so focused on my career and engrossed with the advancement of the APIA political movement, I missed out on many stages of my daughter's childhood before she left for college. I can never recapture those years where I chose my career and causes over my responsibilities as a mother to my only child, and this guilt will always be with me.

Luckily, I married a man who became both mother and father to Stephanie and was the source of stability in the family. His inner strength and resolve to make sure Stephanie had a semblance of normal life even though her mom was MIA ("missing in action") was the saving grace in the marriage and family.

As Ron would say, "Living with Maeley is like living in a three-ring circus. Unfortunately, Stephanie and I are only in one ring."

Despite my transgression, Stephanie has emerged as an amazing young woman and mother herself. She did not want her son, my only grandson, to miss out on a mother/child relationship like she did and took some unusual steps in her own successful career with the private technology sector by limiting herself to job options that would not interfere with time with her son, Max. She understood what it was like to grow up with a career mom. Now, with my grandson soon leaving for college, Stephanie is still young enough to seek professional fulfillment, as she will have complete freedom to continue climbing that professional ladder. She did it the right way.

I decided to retire from my full-time professional career as soon as Max was born in 2002. It was my time to help raise my one and only grandchild, which in turn allowed me to be the mother I wish I could have been to Stephanie.

Today, I advise young career women moving up the ladder that it is a tough balancing act when it comes to family and career, and each person makes personal choices. As for me, I now realize that achievements and titles are there for you at any stage of your life, but the years you miss being a mother is time certain and can never be replaced.

...

I've been encouraged time and time again to run for local office or state office because of my enormous political network and yet I resisted for two reasons.

My husband, who already was carrying the load of raising our daughter and keeping the home fire burning, was against my running for office. And, during this early stage of my life, I too did not have the courage to run for office because I suffered from the same cultural barrier faced by many APIA, the fear of failure. I also could not fathom the thought of asking people for money and then disappointing those donors by losing. Because of my own vulnerability, I have the deepest respect for all the courageous APIA candidates who take the public risk to run for elected office. Now that my time has passed, I try to encourage candidates to overcome the barriers I placed on myself. This is why I am so willing to help APIA candidates with advice and counsel whenever they ask.

The APIA Joint Legislative Caucus Institute's Capitol Academy was developed to help candidates face these cultural barriers and develop the right skills to be competitive candidates for elected office. John Chiang's willingness to give up a safe four years as state treasurer to become the first serious APIA candidate to run for governor was a "profile in courage" because of the odds he faced in this campaign. But the odds he faced were worth it, making the statement that this generation of APIA are no longer content to just have a seat at the table: APIA now want to be at the head of the table.

...

While I was busy running around making a name for myself professionally and politically, my husband, Ron, was the only person who knew deep down how much of my insatiable drive to accomplish was self-driven. People saw me as the epitome of self-confidence and self-assurance because of the recognition I received for my achievements. But it was never enough for me. As Ron would say, there is never a cause or crusade Maeley can turn down. It wasn't until I turned 50 that I realized I had spent most of my life constantly seeking validation of my self-worth through other people's eyes. I didn't really experience a sense of personal worth until I came to accept that the only person I needed to please and respect was myself. Crossing this threshold of self- validation was life changing and liberating.

...

During this chapter of my life, I value time and good health. When I say I need to see a sick friend or spend some time with someone meaningful I have not seen for a while, I try to just "do it." Looking back, I wish I had that same type of urgency years ago.

I was extremely close to Matt Fong, the former California state treasurer and March Fong Eu's son, who was like my little brother. When he was going through his last stage of cancer, I wish I had made more of an effort to visit him in his home in Pasadena. His wife, Paula, called one day to let me know Matt was asking to see me. John Chiang, who was then state treasurer, and I immediately went to see him together. Matt just wanted to chat about what we needed to do during our lifetime as APIA politicos, and his last words to me were to finish this book. John and I only had a limited time with him because of his frail and weak condition. Matt died a few days later, and there was so much more I wanted to say to him, if only I had taken the time.

Former California Assembly Speaker and Lt. Governor Leo McCarthy was someone I owed my career to. He was always there when I needed him during the Asian campaign finance scandal. For some reason I was unable to make it to his funeral service. To this day, I cannot recall why I missed his service. I realize no reason was good enough for me not to pay tribute to someone who meant so much to me personally and professionally.

So, the words, "taking the time," have become a new personal mantra.

...

Could I have been a better role model for women in the Capitol during my era?

Yes, I was able to break the glass ceiling as the first female and first minority chief administrative officer of the Assembly. But I never once questioned whether my salary was comparable to what the former male CAO's were compensated. Perhaps I preferred not to know so I would not be in a position to "make waves."

Did I fight hard enough to protect the women who were subject to sexual harassment in their workplace, even though I was told "hands off" because this was a "member to member" issue? Could I have been more forceful in encouraging these women to seek legal counsel outside the Capitol to protect their rights in the workplace? Not one female adhered to this suggestion when I offered it because they simply did not want to lose their jobs in the Capitol. This was the 70s and 80s, and to see what is now happening with the #MeToo movement demonstrates how many decades it has taken to finally publicly confront this problem of sexual harassment in the political workplace. Bravo to the brave women who led the charge.

. . .

As I was growing in my professional career as a manager, executive, and leader, I had to learn the difference between listening and waiting for my turn to speak. Phil Isenberg, the former assemblyman and mayor of Sacramento, caught me during one of our conversations when I was seeking his advice. He simply said in a quiet, gentle tone, "You are not listening, Maeley." It took me aback because I thought I was, but my body language demonstrated that I was simply waiting my turn to respond to the conversation. His words constantly remind me that one learns more by listening than talking.

BREAST CANCER

"Time for another mammogram," my cheerful general practitioner, Dr. Candace Lawson, said as I was finishing up my 2016 annual checkup.

I took my mammogram slip and casually put it on my desk at home to remind me to make an appointment.

At 74 years old, I took my good health for granted, and delayed scheduling the procedure for a couple of months to accommodate my hectic schedule. I had the minor aches and pains that come with senior status, including mild arthritis in the knees and occasional back aches. At this stage of my life, I was more concerned about my memory and weight.

Being married to a former pharmacist, I took my vitamin supplements and fiber pills and watched my cholesterol and blood pressure. Ron and I laugh about the fact that as we age our bottles of supplements and vitamins increase steadily. Ironically, I commented to Ron on the way to my mammogram that I never was concerned about the results and took it for granted that they would be clean. But as I age, I become more anxious about such procedures.

As the mammogram was underway, I noticed the technician repeating the procedure on my right breast. I didn't think too much about it; the technicians are so professional it's hard to tell what they are seeing on the screen.

A couple of days later I got a call from Capitol Imagery, and a very poised, gentle voice told me that they would like me to come back, this time for another screening and an ultrasound. This was the first time I felt something might be wrong. I couldn't wait to tell Ron, hoping he would reassure me. But I could tell by his calm and stoic reaction that he was concerned as well.

When I returned for the second screening, I noticed they put me in a different waiting room. The lab techs were very kind and thoughtful, recognizing the stress women feel during this first signal that something could be wrong.

As I waited in the ultrasound room for the results, I thought about what to expect: I knew if the technician came through the door, I was ok, but if a doctor came through the door, I was in trouble. When a Dr. Chan came in, my heart dropped as she ordered an additional ultrasound. I asked that my husband be allowed to come in because I knew Ron would know what to ask if there was a problem. Dr. Chan indicated there was a tumor the size of a pencil eraser in my right breast and a biopsy would be needed. She tried to reassure me that the tumor was small and there were no signs it had spread. Ever the optimist, I was hoping the tumor would be benign, but one never escapes the gnawing feeling that it could be malignant.

As anyone who has gone through such an experience can attest, waiting for the biopsy results seems like an eternity. Dr. Lawson was on leave, so a resident called to tell me they found two types of cells in my tumor. Ron and I were confused about what we heard, or maybe we simply did not want to believe it. At our request, another doctor called to explain that my tumor contained both benign and malignant cells. The next step would be for me to select a surgeon.

...

I was still in a state of shock and wanted to share the news with my daughter and my closest circle of friends, including a breast cancer survivor. I also asked Stephanie not to share the diagnosis with my grandson, Max, because he had just lost his paternal grandfather to cancer.

The best advice I received was from my lifelong friend, Dorinda Ng, a former medical assistant to a surgeon, who told me, "Get off the computer and stop doing your own research because it will only cause you more anxiety." She was right. Spending hours doing research online only fed my fears.

Ron, whom I always relied on as the health expert in the family, was himself a bit dazed and, for the first time in our marriage, I could also tell he was scared for me.

My surgeon, Dr. Joyce Eaker, took a direct, no-nonsense approach to my situation that I found professional and comforting. I knew I was in the hands of one of the best breast cancer surgeons in town.

We had a trip to Hawaii scheduled for the following week and wondered if we should cancel so I could have the surgery as soon as possible. Dr. Eaker assured me there was no need to rush; the tumor was very small and slow growing. The Hawaii trip gave us a brief reprieve from our stress and anxiety. I had never seen Ron scared, and we had both taken my good health for granted. I tried to stay stoic as I awaited surgery. I did not want to allow myself to break down; I needed to be strong for Ron as well. I had no fear. I thought that if I could give birth to Stephanie, I could do this.

Four hours after surgery on May 2nd, I was on my way home with only a slight soreness in the breast area and under my arms where they took out two lymph nodes to determine if there were any cancer cells undetected by the ultrasound. This was our greatest fear, and we asked Dr. Eaker to let us know the results as soon as possible. Thanks to the Reiki treatments I received from my friend in the Bay Area, Sandy Wong, who specializes in Body Talk, I required no pain pills after surgery and felt fine.

Dr. Eaker called two days later with the most welcome news: no cells had been detected in the surrounding tissue and the lymph nodes were clean. Ron's sobs of relief released all the emotions he was repressing through this journey with me. He confessed that his greatest concern had been that my cancer cells had spread to the lymph nodes with the possibility of migrating throughout my body.

I was looking forward to meeting the two oncologists referred to me by my friend, Bobbie Metzger, who is also a breast cancer survivor. Dr. Janice Ryu and Dr. Rohat Rohatgi, along with Dr. Eaker, were Sutter Health's breast cancer dream team. I was delighted to have them as my doctors.

Dr. Ryu and Dr. Rohatgi recommended three weeks of radiation and an estrogen blocker to help prevent growth of my specific type of cancer. I wanted to do everything possible to prevent a recurrence. I was so lucky, but I didn't want to further tempt Lady Luck. My tests have been clean for three years, and I now belong to the breast cancer victim sisterhood. The experience was a vivid reminder of how precious life is.

AGING

"The longer I live, the more beautiful life becomes."
— Frank Lloyd Wright

Becoming a breast cancer survivor was a life changing experience because it made me face my age and mortality like never before.

Before this episode I took so much for granted in life, as if I were going to live forever. My retirement life was filled with constant activities with family, serving on boards, participating in community and political events, enjoying friends, and having the freedom to travel anywhere in the world. The best part of retirement is that you can choose who you want to see, where you want to go, and whether a social engagement is worth putting yourself together to leave the house. As they say, learning how to retire gracefully is simply to enjoy the passage and embrace the joy of gratitude.

I am so lucky to have found Ron, a soulmate for life, who stuck by me through my insecurities of constantly trying to prove I was worthy, through my times as an absentee mother and wife, and still loved me enough to hang around for 50 years.

During my 17 years of retirement I have tried to make up for the time I lost with my daughter, Stephanie, by helping her raise my grandson, Max. Stephanie, who felt the pressure of living in my shadow growing up, finished college with a master's degree, and from there her professional and leadership accomplishments soared in the field of technology. She now commands her own identity in the community and professionally so that she is no longer seen as Ron and Maeley's daughter; we are now identified as Stephanie Tom's parents.

My only grandchild, 17-year-old Max, is a year away from college and recently received a four-year scholarship to play baseball at Kansas University. I cherish my 17 years watching him grow, and to this day the sight of him makes my heart sing.

I look around to where I am today—with a family of my own including Stephanie's partner Stuart who is like a son, my stepson Darren and his wife Diana and a large circle of loving nieces and nephews from the Tom side of the family—and I feel complete. They have replaced the missed family presence of my own childhood.

Friendships continue to be so important to me. As Ron would say, "Maeley doesn't lose friends, she simply adds friends. And if you ever do a favor for Maeley, she spends the rest of her life trying to repay the favor." To this day I keep in touch and cherish all the networks of friends who have graced my life.

I had career opportunities that challenged me as an Asian American woman and yet allowed me to break through some glass ceilings professionally and politically. More important, my career provided me a gift to help my own ethnic community achieve a voice in mainstream politics and, hopefully, inspire individuals to believe in themselves and their potential.

I continue to have the zest and curiosity to see how I can keep growing and learning each new day. I continue to share my experiences and mentor those who seek my guidance and advice.

APIA are steadily growing as a political force, but there are still more barriers and ceilings that need to break for APIA to be taken seriously for their talent and leadership skills in this country dominated by a western culture that traditionally listens to those who shout the loudest.

This is why I enjoy helping organizations such as the Asian Pacific Islander American Public Affairs Association (APAPA), founded by entrepreneur and businessman C.C. Yin, whose passion and dedication is to help new immigrants flourish and empower themselves in this country by being active in civic engagement, becoming leaders in all professions, and participating in the electoral process.

In February, 2019, I received an invitation to become a member of the Committee 100, a non-profit leadership organization of prominent and extraordinary Chinese Americans in business, government, academia, and the arts, founded by the late world-famous architect I.M. Pei and internationally acclaimed cellist Yo-Yo Ma, among others.

In addition to its commitment to promoting the full participation of Chinese Americans in all aspects of American life and constructive relations between the United States and Greater China, it is dedicated to next-generation leadership building.

When I look back to see where I came from and how I got to where I am today, how can I not be grateful?

I don't view getting old as a coming to the end phase. Instead I now see every healthy day as a gift for me to pursue an opportunity to learn and grow and an opportunity to make a positive difference somewhere, somehow.

As I reflect on my life, I realize that it does not matter how you start out, but how you end up that really counts. And I end this book with a closure that signifies how I tried to live my life: "The happiest people don't necessarily have the best of everything; they just make the most of everything that comes their way."

My greatest gift to myself is finally accepting who I am today. And now, maybe you, too, know who I am.

Stephanie and Ron: From back to front: Stuart, Ron, Darren, Diana, Stephanie, Jared, and Maxwell; Ron, Maxwell, Stuart, and Stephanie

APPENDIX

TRIBUTES

The two APIA Democratic leadership conferences in 1982 and 1987 made history by uniting the different Asian Pacific Islander American sub-ethnic groups, resulting in a unified platform to engage gubernatorial and presidential candidates in publicly addressing issues critical to this voter base.

This effort brought together individuals who were champions and trailblazers during an era when our communities were fighting for a presence and a voice in this country. It was an honor to work with these leaders, whose blood, sweat, and tears made these events a reality.

It was also a privilege to write a column for Asian Week, one of the first Asian English-language publications in the country, published by the Fang family in San Francisco. I have reprinted two of my personal favorite columns.

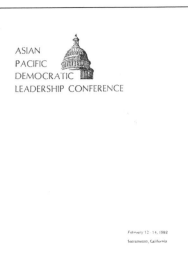

ASIAN
PACIFIC
DEMOCRATIC
LEADERSHIP CONFERENCE

February 12–14, 1982
Sacramento, California

Maeley Tom, State Chair

Georgette Imura,
No. Vice Chair

Collin Lai, So. Vice Chair

Wilson Chang, Treasurer

Glenn Barroga, So. Secretary

Fely Horanzy, No. Secretary

Not Pictured: Ying Lee Kelley, Secretary

CALIFORNIA ASIAN PACIFIC DEMOCRATIC
LEADERSHIP CONFERENCE 1982
STEERING COMMITTEE AND PARTICIPANTS

San Francisco:
Alice Bulos
Tim Dayonot
Henry Der
Wendy Ho
Thomas Hsieh
Tom Kim
Bob Kiyota
Louis Hop Lee
Tom Kim
Stella Kiyota
Lim P. Lee
Jeff Mori
Phil Nakamura
Jadine Nielsen
Margine Sako
Lillian Sing
Jim Sing
Steve Shon
Ed Tong
Yori Wada
Larry Wong
Harold Yee

Los Angeles:
Kevin Acebo
Annie Cho
Sue Embrey
Matthew Kim Fong
Mas Fukai
Fred Fujioka
Irene Hirano

Royal Morales
Debbie Nakatomi
Dennis Nishikawa
Audrey Noda
Rose Ochi
Lonnie Sakoda
Tong Sung
Tritia Toyota
Chris Ung
Lynn Choy Uyeda
Ron Wakabayashi
Peter Wiersma
Mike Woo
Gay Yuen Wong
Mike Yamaki

Fresno:
Celese Don
Tony and Jeanette
Ishii
Harry Kubo

Bay area:
Bill Hing
Ying Lee Kelley
Floyd Mori
Dr. Raj Prasad
Dr. Allan Seid
Tong Suhr

Orange County:
Michael Huyhn
Gloria Julagay

**Sacramento/
Stockton:**
Morris Artiaga
Larry Asera
Tom Chinn
Harriet Fukushima
Dr. Ferd Galvez
Gladys Ikeda;
Chewy Ito
Emiko Kawasaki
Dean Lan
Dick Lew
Satoshi Matsuda
Tom Nakashima
Gloria Megina Ochoa
Dale Shimasaki
Karen Sonoda
David Takashima
Ron Tom
Jackie Tsang
Rene Uda
Elena Wong
Darrell Woo
Karen Yamamoto
Linda Tsao Yang

The
NATIONAL DEMOCRATIC COUNCIL
of
ASIAN & PACIFIC AMERICANS

presents

Hyatt at Los Angeles Airport
CALIFORNIA

October
16, 17, 18
1987

Barbara Miyamoto, Co-Chair

Maeley Tom, Co-Chair

Ginger Lew, Founding Chair

Susan Lee, Executive Director

Daphne Kwok,
Administrative Assistant

THE NATIONAL DEMOCRATIC COUNCIL OF ASIAN & PACIFIC AMERICANS
THE MARGIN OF VICTORY, OCT. 16-18 1987
STEERING COMMITTEE AND PARTICIPANTS

Interim Board of Directors:
Kevin Acebo
Rajen Anand
Patricia Kohokuhealani Brandt
Alice Bulos
Cedric Chao
Margaret Chin
Bill Chong
Kanak Dutta
Michael Eng
Ross Harano
Irene Hirano
Georgette Imura
Tom Kim
Steven Lam
Louis Hop Lee
Virginia Lee
Ginger Lew
Tin-Mala
Sandra Mori
Jadine Nielsen
Rajen Prasad
Lani Sakoda
James Shimoura
Dolores Sibonga
Linda Tsao Yang
Ronald Wakabashi

Northern California:
Sandra Mori–
 Co-Chair
Louis Hop Lee–
 Co-Chair
Alice Bulos
Gigi Carriel
Cedric Chao
Ed dela Cruz
Henry Der
Tom Kim
Richard Lew
Rod McLeod
David Nakayama
Zoon Nguyen
Allan Seid
Vu-Duc Vuong
Leland Yee

Pacific Islander:
Andy Ahpo
Jim Kahue

Los Angeles:
Bert Nakano–Chair
Rajen Anand
Alan Chou
Tommy Chung
Mike Eng
Gerald Gubatan

Victor Huey
Miya Iwataki
Bill Kaneko
Diana Kang
David Kim
Collin Lai
Edward Lee
C.H. Lee
Janet Lim
Steven Ling
Akito Maehara
Jim Miyano
Royal Morales
Audrey Noda
Mary Nishimoto
Dennis Nishikawa
Tony Ricasa
Lani Sakoda
Terry Terauchi
Meg Thornton
Christine Ung
Kaz Umemoto
Alan Woo
Joselyn Yap

Convention Committees Platform:
Steve Arevelo–Chair
Anthony Chang
Wilson Chang

Michael Chou
Pauline Chu
Tong Soo Chung
Henry Der
Tom Eng
Marina Hsieh
Jackie Huey
Brij Khare
Dan Lam
Irene Lee
Elaine Lew
Janet Lim
Robert Machida
Audrey Noda
Sharon Paulo
Tom Pok
Vince Reyes
Bob Santos
Parvi Syal
Art Song
Alicia Wang
Jocelyn Yap
Leland Yee

Washington, D.C.:
Sumiko Biderman
Gloria Caoile
John Chiang
Franklin Chow
Rose Chu
Patricia Fenn
William Himel
Alice Huckaby
Kris Ikejiri
Earl Ing
Bruce King

Endora King
Victor King
Irene Lee
Mee Y. Lee
Lin Liu
Wil Luna
Sandy Lwin
Tin-Mala
Hope Nakamaura
Kathy Lo Peterson
John Trasvina
Anne Uno
Geoffrey Why
Marion Yip
Ling Yu
Robert Zung

Rules:
Gloria Caoile–Chair
Jan Allianic
Andy Anh
James Fang
Grace Hing
Puni Hokea
Roland Kotani
Kashore Kripilani
Carl Lindstrom
Allan Seid
Veda Thakur

By-Laws:
Andrew Sun–Chair
Sumiko Biderman
Lita David
Patricia Fenn
Victor Hsi

Collin Lai
Marivic Manibag
Nirmal Mishra
Jeff Mori
Monda Pasquel
Tom Surh
Vacant Telang
Vu-Duc Vuong
Art Wanga

ASIAN WEEK, April 26, 1991

My Mother, My Self

Capitol Watch · Maeley Tom

Throughout my years in politics, many have asked how my background and upbringing have influenced my decision to go into politics. Because I did not grow up in a traditional Asian American family setting, I was under no influence to pursue any particular career goal. Thus, I fell into politics quite by accident.

My parents were members of the Cantonese Opera troupe that immigrated to this country in the 40s when this form of entertainment was at its height of popularity in Chinatown neighborhoods. I was born at the Chinese Hospital in San Francisco which was conveniently located next to the building that housed all the entertainers.

My father, a very popular comedian, subsequently returned to Hong Kong without me and my mother when I was 4 years old. He never returned, and eventually suffered a fatal heart attack in Canton, China. During my early childhood, my mother sang in local gambling dens to support the both of us. In order for her to pursue this type of life, I was placed in a home in the Richmond District and was raised by a French Basque family.

If it were not for the weekend visits to Chinatown, I would not have had any Asian identity at that time. Visiting San Francisco Chinatown with my parents and their friends was like visiting a foreign country.

My parents' peers spoke only Chinese, dressed differently, ate different foods, and exhibited living habits that were totally foreign to me. However, in order to survive during these weekends, I was forced to learn to speak Chinese and gradually became acclimated to their way of life. To this day I cherish these childhood memories and realize these experiences have helped me to gain a deeper appreciation of my Chinese heritage.

I learned to understand that while my parents physically moved to this country, they and their peers resisted any efforts to acclimate to the American way of life or speak a language different than their native tongue. The Chinatown environment made it unnecessary for them to learn to live otherwise. As the new wave of Asian immigrants came into his county, I continued to see this same pattern of attitudes and behavior exhibited by the elderly immigrant population who, when given the choice, would choose to live within their own Chinese community neighborhoods.

My mother refused to leave New York Chinatown to return to California to be with me and my family, even though I would have been able to provide her with more comfortable living conditions. Instead, she preferred to work as a waitress in New York Chinatown and live in a crowded tenement building to be close to her Chinese opera friends. She did not want to leave her mah jongg games, the Chinese restaurants, markets and businesses, and a way of life that did not require her to ever venture beyond the boundaries of her neighborhood.

Clearly my mother and I lived in two separate worlds. Even when we did see one another, our ability to communicate was hampered by language barriers. My limited Cantonese only allowed me to conduct casual conversations with my mother.

In fact, she never quite understood what I did for a living because I was not in a traditional profession that was revered by the Chinese community. She did not comprehend nor share my interest in Asian issues. Although she did understand I worked for a "politician," she was never able to distinguish if my boss was a mayor, governor, or even president of the U.S. One time she thought I worked for President Reagan when I was appointed to his Commission on Women Business Ownership until I clarified this appointment through an interpreter friend.

As the years rolled by, I learned to appreciate and accept my mother for living her life the best way she knew how. As a dutiful Chinese daughter I could not escape the need and desire to feel some sense of approval or hear some words of praise from my mother, but I never found the appropriate words or time to ever discuss this need with her. Or, maybe I was just embarrassed to ask.

My mother passed away two weeks ago. I felt the loss very deeply because we had so little time together. The thought stayed with me as I went through her belongings and found a scrapbook that contained articles about me. Most of the articles were written in English...but, she chose to keep them anyway.

By her bedside, I found two recent Chinese language newspaper articles announcing my appointment as Senator Roberti's administrative director. Her closest friend told me that she kept the articles close by during her last days to show friends who visited her.

Somehow that simple message ended my quest and made my loss more bearable. As all dutiful Chinese daughters and sons learn to understand, no achievement in life is greater than giving one's honorable mother pride and honor.

I dedicate this article to my mother, Lee Chor Fun.

ASIAN WEEK, March 26, 1993

A Special Lincoln School Reunion

Capitol Watch · Maeley Tom

Recently, I was excited to return to Oakland to reunite with classmates who graduated from Lincoln Elementary and Jr. High School during the years 1952-54. Lincoln School in the early 50s was 80 percent Asian and served as the focal center for the Chinese community neighborhood that surrounded the School.

The area I lived in during those days could be described as an inner-city neighborhood encircling the existing Chinatown area, which has since expanded tenfold. Most of the parents of my neighborhood peers immigrated to this county in the 40s. Thus, most of my classmates were born in the United States like myself, growing up in a bicultural environment. At home, parents spoke Chinese, cooked Chinese meals, and tried to maintain some semblance of Chinese cultural traditions. However, at school, we were just like any other American teen-agers.

There were no language barriers; we spoke the same American slang. Our dress, interests, hobbies, and social patterns were as Americanized as they come. In addition, Lincoln School had a playground across the street called Lincoln Square, where many of us gathered after school or during the weekends.

There was one Chinese teacher at Lincoln by the name of Bob Walton Lee, who eventually rose through the administrative ranks to become one of the first Chinese principals in the Oakland School District. He was our role model, and committed his time and energy to organizing social, athletic, and community activities that provided us with a positive social structure. During this time, there were no Asian gangs in our inner-city neighborhood, and delinquency and criminal incidents were rare.

Most of the parents living in the area earned modest incomes as owners of small businesses, primarily in Chinatown, or worked in service-oriented jobs as waiters, grocers, etc. Successful professional Asian families did not stay in this inner-city neighborhood, but instead chose to live in East Oakland, Berkeley, or the Alameda suburb area.

It was not unusual for many of my schoolmates to either rush home to help with the family business or baby-sit younger children until the parents came home. On top of this, many of us attended two hours of Chinese school after regular school, which was another social outlet for us. Life seemed so simple and uncomplicated then. There were three options that faced us at Lincoln School: 1) attend college after high school, 2) graduate and go into the family business, or 3) go to a technical school such as Lancy College to develop a trade profession—simple as that.

The social structure and security of growing up in a predominantly Asian neighborhood where everyone spoke the same language and socialized on a common level with other teenagers of Anglo or non-Asian ethnic descent, was taken for granted by us. We were Asian, but felt little difference from our non-Asian peers. Lincoln School and its neighborhood provided us with the best of both worlds—a sense of appreciation for our Asian culture and ethnic identity and, at the time, the opportunity to be a part of mainstream America as Americans.

The tradition of academic achievement among Asians was very evident even during these years. In reviewing my Lincoln School reunion book, I am proud to say that, despite struggling economic conditions, 50 percent of my classmates went on to college. But, even more impressive is the pride my classmates shared regarding their children's achievements. Approximately 80 percent of my classmates' children are either established in professional positions or attend college. This statistic is a tribute to the legacy of Lincoln School.

My Lincoln School classmates and I were indeed fortunate to be born and raised here during a time when racial divisiveness was not a major issue. During those days we didn't see ourselves as Chinese or Asian. We saw ourselves as Americans.

Unfortunately, our youth today are not allowed to enjoy the same luxury. The competition among ethnic minorities for diminishing resources, the dominance of the Pacific Rim trade deficit, and the influx of Asian immigrants during the last decade has created an environment of racial intolerance, jealousies and scapegoating for our community. The lack of resources to help the vast number of new immigrants assimilate to our American society has also maximized our problems.

Therefore, the young generation of today can no longer enjoy the mere simple existence as everyday Americans, as we did during the Lincoln School days. Today's world does not permit it. We need to help provide this generation the same opportunities to succeed and realize the American Dream, by becoming more politically involved and more vocal about problems this generation faces. Perhaps the day will come, in this country, when all Asians will not have to be identified as Asian Pacific American, but just "plain ol' Americans" like the Lincoln School days.

Thank you to the following classmates who pulled the reunion event together: Florence Chin Louie, Rose Chin Hong, Judy Chu Porter, Charmaine Eng Ngin, Gene Roh, Ellsie Yee Wilkic, Stanley Gin Chin, Stanley H. Chin, and Darlene Joe Lee.

I dedicate this article to my Lincoln School buddies: Gerry Oh, Lainey Wong, Sarah Watkins, Lucy Ozawa, Lonnie Wong, and Elaine "Ditto" Wong.

RESOURCES

Lungren:
(1988, February). Quiet minority shifts tactics in California: appointee battle reflects Asian American power. *Washington Post*

Kennedy/Simpson:
Tom, M. (1989, July). Lobbying on Capitol Hill, and Kennedy/Simpson immigration reform Act. *Asian Week*

Scandal:
Brauchli, M. (1997, May). Asian political money flowed in California before D.C. found it. *Wall Street Journal*

O'Rourke, L. (1997, July). Sacramentan says Huang ties misleading. *Sacramento Bee*

Gladstone, M. (1997, July). Fundraising scandal drags insider in the limelight. *L.A. Times*

Smith, D. (1997, August). Capitol insider on hot seat. *Sacramento Bee*

(1997, August). Support letters to the editor. *Sacramento Bee*

Miller, A. and Gladstone, M. (1997, July). Letter details plan for Asian business to meet Clinton staff. *LA Times*

ABOUT THE AUTHOR

 Born in San Francisco Chinatown to a family of Chinese Opera celebrities ill-suited to raising a daughter, Maeley made her own way through most of her youth, lonely and full of self-doubt. But adversity instilled in her the self-reliance and confidence that eventually made her an exceptional political force.

Asian Week newspaper called her "one of the most powerful and influential non-elected political figures in the Asian American community" during an era when Asian Americans were struggling to find a voice in politics and public policy.

During her 20-year career in the California State Legislature she broke the glass ceiling twice, as the first woman Chief Administrative Officer of the Assembly and the first ethnic minority woman to become Chief of Staff to the Senate Pres. Pro Tem. Her access to political influence motivated her to empower the largely silent Asian American constituency by creating institutions and events to inspire engagement in the political process.

Revered as the "Godmother of Asian American politics," she continues to mentor scores of young Asian Americans who seek careers in politics or public service. She is married to Dr. Ronald Tom, Pharm. D, and has a daughter, Stephanie, and grandson, Max.

Made in the USA
San Bernardino, CA
24 June 2020